"*The Nordstrom Way: The Inside Story of America's #1 Customer Service Company* takes an unusual look at the direct link between empowering your employees and creating a long-term sustainable relationship with your customers. More businesses should follow their example."
—Howard Schultz
Chairman and Chief Executive Officer
Starbucks Coffee Company

"The book documents in rich detail the marvelous ingredients in the stew that makes the Nordstrom Way so outstandingly successful. It hammers home the underlying truth: You must make the decision to trust people as customers and as employees. This pervades every aspect of Nordstrom described in this very readable book."
—Donald E. Petersen
Retired Chairman, Ford Motor Co.

"The phrase 'Nordstrom is planning a store here' can send a local retail community into a cold sweat. *The Nordstrom Way: The Inside Story of America's #1 Customer Service Company* tells how this upscale Seattle retailer became the feared and admired powerhouse of modern retailing."
—Ron Zemke
Coauthor of *Managing Knock Your Socks Off Service* and *ServiceAmerica!*

"The success of Nordstrom is still the best evidence of the notion that customer service makes money. This book tells how it works!"
—Peter Glen
Author of *It's Not My Department*

The
NORDSTROM
Way

The

NORDSTROM

THE INSIDE STORY
OF AMERICA'S #1 *Way*
CUSTOMER SERVICE COMPANY

Robert Spector
Patrick D. McCarthy

John Wiley & Sons, Inc.

New York • Chichester • Brisbane • Toronto • Singapore

HF
5415
.5
S62
.1995

A portion of Patrick McCarthy's royalty earnings will be donated to a charitable fund for children.

This text is printed on acid-free paper.

Copyright © 1995 by Robert Spector and Patrick D. McCarthy
Published by John Wiley & Sons, Inc.

This publication is designed to provide accurate and authoritative
information in regard to the subject matter covered. It is sold
with the understanding that the publisher is not engaged in
rendering legal, accounting, or other professional services. If
legal advice or other expert assistance is required, the services
of a competent professional person should be sought.

Library of Congress Cataloging-in-Publication Data:

Spector, Robert, 1947—
    The Nordstrom way : the inside story of America's #1 customer
service company / by Robert Spector and Patrick D. McCarthy.
        p.   cm.
    Includes index.
    ISBN 0-471-58496-7 (alk. paper)
        1. Customer service—United States.   2. Nordstrom (Firm)
    3. Department stores—United States.   I. McCarthy, Patrick D.
    II. Title.
    HF5415.5.S627   1995
    658.8¢71—dc20   94-39182

Printed in the United States of America

10   9   8   7   6

In loving memory of my parents,
Fred and Florence Spector,
who taught me The Spector Way:
work hard, be good, do well.

R.S.

In memory of Ray Black,
who first showed me The Nordstrom Way.

P.Mc.

Acknowledgments

The names on an authors' page cannot accurately reflect the number of people who helped make this book possible. Deep and heartfelt thanks go to the following:

Pat McCarthy for envisioning the potential of this project and entrusting me to help him tell it; and for his belief in the Nordstrom way of doing business.

Bruce Nordstrom, Jim Nordstrom, John Nordstrom, and Jack McMillan for their cooperation and trust, and for the use of two privately published family histories, "The Immigrant in 1887" by John W. Nordstrom, and "A Winning Team: The Story of Everett, Elmer & Lloyd Nordstrom" by Elmer Nordstrom.

Kellie Tormey for her service above and beyond the call of duty (this book could not have been done without her) and Alli Sweet, who fulfilled every request with swiftness and a smile.

The many Nordstrom people in sales and management who participated in author interviews and thereby put a human face on the company.

Betsy Sanders for her thoughtful reading of the manuscript.

Ruth Mills and John Mahaney of John Wiley & Sons, who believed in this project, and Danalyn Adams for all her help.

Elizabeth Wales, agent extraordinaire, who served as editor, sounding board, mother hen (that's not sexist, is it, Elizabeth?), taskmaster, and, most importantly, friend.

Bob Spitz for his sage advice about the publishing business.

My sisters, Sandra Goldberg and Barbara Eisner, for always being there.

And Marybeth and Fae Spector, who sustained me every day in every way.

Robert Spector
Seattle, Washington

Contents

Introduction

The idea of telling the Nordstrom customer service story was born on March 18, 1990, when Elizabeth Wales, a Seattle literary agent, gazed out the back window of her home, where she saw her neighbor, Patrick McCarthy, mowing his backyard lawn. Earlier that same day, Wales had read a lengthy feature story on McCarthy in the *Seattle Times*. The article, which ran under the headline "Personal Touch: Service Makes Salesman a Legend at Nordstrom," examined McCarthy's reputation as the retail chain's quintessential employee, the top sales associate for fifteen consecutive years. While Wales, whose spouse is a McCarthy customer, was reading about McCarthy's willingness to make deliveries to the homes of his customers, an amusing image flashed in her head: "One of these days, Patrick is going to come home with my husband's pants."

In a sense, McCarthy's personally delivering those pants is the perfect metaphor for the Nordstrom way. Nordstrom's culture encourages entrepreneurial, motivated men and women to make the extra effort to give customer service that is unequalled in American retailing. "Not service like it used to be, but service that never was," marveled correspondent Morley Safer on a *60 Minutes*

1

Nordstrom profile. "A place where service is an act of faith." But Nordstrom's standard is not limited to retailing. "If all businesses could be like Nordstrom and all employees could be like Pat McCarthy," said Harry Mullikin, chairman emeritus of Westin Hotels and Resorts, "it would change the whole economy of this country."

At Nordstrom, at least, there are many thousands of employees like Pat McCarthy in company stores all over America, and the reader will meet several of them in these pages. In fact, one of the reasons that Nordstrom—the family and the company—agreed to cooperate on this book was our commitment to not focus exclusively on McCarthy (who is quoted in this narrative in the third person), but also to include the comments and experiences of other top Nordstrom sales and management people. We later added the observations of several members of the company's board of directors, as well as prominent business leaders who happen to be Nordstrom customers.

Most importantly, co-chairmen Bruce A. Nordstrom, John N. Nordstrom, James F. Nordstrom, and John A. "Jack" McMillan participated in a series of candid interviews, together and separately, with Robert Spector. The result of their cooperation is an unprecedented study of every detail that makes Nordstrom work.

It should be noted that Nordstrom did not suggest that this book be written nor did the company commission its publication. In fact, as a rule, Nordstrom executives at all levels of the organization rarely grant interviews—even when they are being honored. When Bruce Nordstrom was selected as *Footwear News Magazine's* Man of the Year for 1987, he reluctantly accepted the award, but politely declined to be interviewed for the article. The Nordstroms aren't snobs; it's just that they are uncomfortable with blowing their own horn. They like to say that there is nothing special or magical or difficult about what they do and that the system is embarrassingly simple. "We outservice, not outsmart," is a typical Nordstromism. They describe themselves as "just shoe salesmen" who haven't been educated at the elite business schools of Harvard or Stanford, but rather at the University of Washington (which has a solid reputation of its own). James Nordstrom once conceded to *Footwear News* that, "Many people think that we Nordstroms are secretive, because we don't talk much about ourselves. The truth is, we can't afford to boast. If we did, we might start to believe our own stories, get big heads and stop trying. . . . Our success is simply a matter of service, selection, fair pricing, hard work, and plain luck."

Such self-effacing comments might be dismissed as disingenuous if not for the fact that the Nordstroms' history confirms their desire not to draw attention to themselves. Although they are extremely competitive, they prefer to project an image of small-town modesty. Ann D. McLaughlin, the former U.S. Secretary of Labor, who has been a Nordstrom director since 1992, recalled that when she flew from her home in Washington, D.C., to Seattle for a board meeting, the Nordstrom family, "thanked me for taking the time to come. It wouldn't have occurred to me to be thanked for doing something I feel responsible for. But that's their attitude. The boardroom is very low key and that helps keep everyone in perspective." When the Nordstrom family controlled the ownership of the Seattle Seahawks of the National Football League, they sought a degree of anonymity that is almost unheard of in a business where owners often battle their players for a share of the limelight. According to Mike McCormack, the former general manager of the Seahawks, the Nordstroms did not even want to have their names and pictures printed in the Seahawks media guide. "There were times when protocol demanded that they make an appearance on the field, to present a check to charity," said McCormack. "They did not like that. They wanted to enjoy it in the background."

Nordstrom people at all levels are especially reticent when it comes to talking about their reputation for customer service because, "We know that, at this moment, someone, somewhere is getting bad service at Nordstrom," said Jammie Baugh, executive vice-president and general manager of the Southern California division, who added, "It was never that we were so great, it was just that everyone else was so bad." Her colleague, Martha S. Wikstrom, general manager of Nordstrom's Capital (Washington, D.C.) region said Nordstrom's reputation for customer service (which was built on word-of-mouth, not self-congratulatory ads or press releases) has put it in a position of being held to a higher standard than its competition. Wikstrom recalled the times when customers, "who have gotten poor service from us told me, 'If this had happened at Macy's, I would expect it, but this is *Nordstrom.*'"

■ The McCarthy Example

This selfless attitude promotes a culture where a person like McCarthy can succeed. In fact, his journey to financial rewards and job satisfaction can serve as an example, not only for every one of Nordstrom's 35,000 employees, but also for every frontline employee in virtually any business.

For 15 consecutive years, from 1977 through 1991, McCarthy was the number one sales person in the chain. In 1992, 1993, and 1994 he was runner-up to Leslie Kaufman of the Westside store in Los Angeles (who we will meet later in this book). McCarthy sells well over one million dollars worth of merchandise each year in the men's clothing department of the downtown

Seattle flagship store. With commissions, McCarthy can earn upwards of $90,000, plus profit sharing and other benefits—not bad for someone who is paid a base wage of $9.85 an hour. But McCarthy's self image is not that of an hourly employee; like other top Nordstrom sales people, he considers himself an entrepreneurial, independent businessman ("a franchise within a franchise," he calls himself) with a client list of 6,000 names, ranging from recent college graduates shopping for their first suit, to U.S. senators and corporate chief executives (including Nordstrom co-chairmen John, James, and Bruce Nordstrom and Jack McMillan), who rely upon McCarthy to take care of their wardrobe needs.

One of his customers, Jerry Grinstein, chairman and chief executive officer of the Burlington Northern Railroad of Fort Worth, Texas, said, "Pat takes care of me and my whole family. On a trip to New York City, one of our kids said he wanted to shop for a jacket. I said, 'Go see Patrick. He'll make sure you get the right thing.' That ended that discussion. When I'm in Seattle, I will stop off at Nordstrom to say hello to Pat, even when I'm not shopping, because I like him so much. I can trust him to do what he says he's going to do. He can get something ready in an hour when everyone else will take a week. When I asked Pat to get sport jackets for our senior officers, he took care of it in the time he said it was going to take. There was never an excuse, delay, or mishap anywhere along the line."

Grinstein, a Seattle native who has been a McCarthy customer for more than twenty years, marveled at McCarthy's ability to "get into the customer's mind. All of us talk the language of being focused on the customer. But sometimes we become so obsessed by costs that we lose sight of the customer. Pat is thinking of me more than he's thinking of Nordstrom's costs (which is how Nordstrom wants him to think). Once, when I was shopping, Pat asked me if I needed any shirts or ties. I said the only thing I needed were walking shoes. He said they were on sale and that he would pick up a pair for me. I told him my size and he later sent me the pair. When I tried them on and they didn't fit, I sent them back to Pat." The store didn't have Grinstein's size in that style, but instead of losing the sale, McCarthy sent Grinstein a pair in a similar style. Although they were more expensive than the first pair and were *not* on sale, McCarthy still charged Grinstein the sale price of the original purchase. "Now," Grinstein asked rhetorically, "how could I ever go to anybody else?"

The Nordstrom system supports and encourages individual salespeople to have an intimate business dialogue and relationship with the key vendors in their departments. Donald E. Petersen, the retired chairman of Ford Motor Company, recalled the time that he was looking for a particular style of sport coat and asked both McCarthy and a salesman from another top retailer if they could find the coat in a 43 long, which is a hard-to-find size. "In a matter of a day or two, Pat called me back to tell me the coat was on its way to the store, and asked me when I was going to be in Seattle to pick it up. He has that kind of relationship with his suppliers."

McCarthy has the ability to work with several different customers at once, at various stages of the selling process—from welcoming one man entering the department to finding merchandise for a couple of others to consulting with the tailor to closing a sale with yet another customer. "The number of people he can serve simultaneously is phenomenal," Kip Toner, a vice-president of a Seattle auction company and a longtime McCarthy client, told the *Seattle Times*. "He should charge admission. It's a show, like a carefully orchestrated symphony, where he's got them all moving at the same time. And the joy is, everyone's happy."

Nordstrom creates the right conditions for its employees. "A person like Pat McCarthy can blossom in the Nordstrom environment," said Harry Mullikin of Westin Hotels, a McCarthy customer for more than two decades. "But if he went to work for another company, he couldn't—no matter what kind of person he is. Pat has this marvelous ability to make you feel that you're the only customer he has; that you're the only customer he wants to see. He might not see me for a month or two, but when I come back into the store, he acts as if he's been waiting for me all that time." When McCarthy calls Mullikin about the arrival of some new merchandise in the store, "Pat makes it sound as if he has something special just for me—which is not true, of course," Mullikin said with a chuckle.

McCarthy's silky treatment of clients has made him Seattle's best-known sales associate. Even people who have never bought a suit at Nordstrom know who Pat McCarthy is. A breakfast meeting with Pat in a downtown Seattle restaurant is repeatedly interrupted by customers coming over to his table to say hello. He is frequently invited to give speeches about customer service and building a clientele to the sales and marketing teams of law firms, insurance companies, banks, and other businesses.

■ A Career That Almost Never Happened

McCarthy's success is all the more remarkable because, in the early 1970s, after working at Nordstrom for less than two years, he came within a thread of being fired because he had developed a reputation for being uncooperative, hard to manage, and not a team player. Fortunately, the new department manager, who had been ordered to terminate McCarthy, didn't believe in dropping the ax without first forming his own opinion. Besides, he'd been told that McCarthy was a sincere man, who was open and friendly with customers and possessed the potential to be a good Nordstrom sales associate. That department manager, Patrick Kennedy, told McCarthy to stop fighting with co-workers over customers—even at those times when McCarthy was positive that the customer was his. "Ring up the sale for the other guy," said Kennedy, "and smile when you do it." Then he gave McCarthy some of the most important advice a sales associate can get, advice that McCarthy has carried with him ever since, advice that today he gives to new employees: "Relax. Stop worrying about making sales." Easier said than done, thought McCarthy, in the hotly competitive Nordstrom arena of commission sales. But, Kennedy explained, when you stop worrying about money and concentrate on serving the customer, the money will follow. People who succeed in sales understand this paradox.

McCarthy had arrived at Nordstrom from an unlikely situation—the state prison in Shelton, Washington, a timber community sixty miles south of Seattle, where he worked as a counselor for felons. The first couple of years at Shelton, he helped adult criminals make the transition to the community by placing them in jobs; after that, he became supervisor of a halfway house for juveniles, counseling them to stay in school or find employment, rather than remain dependent upon the state. The work was frustrating and mentally draining. "I've always believed in hard work, but in that environment, it just wasn't there. You couldn't get the kid to listen, to understand that you can make something of your life. As much as I wanted to help, I couldn't."

A college friend set up an interview for McCarthy with the friend's father-in-law, Lloyd Nordstrom, one of the co-chairmen of what was then known as Nordstrom Best,

Incorporated. Although Nordstrom was then seventy years old, it had recently diversified into apparel and become a fast-growing, publicly traded company under the management of a new generation of Nordstroms—John, Bruce, and James Nordstrom and Jack McMillan—all in their thirties. The seven-store retail chain was generating annual sales of about $80 million, as well as hundreds of new career-advancement opportunities. Lloyd Nordstrom advised McCarthy to try a career in sales, a field that McCarthy thought he "might have an aptitude for, because I had always been comfortable with people and sensitive to their feelings," he recalled. In January 1971, at the age of twenty-six, with a wife and three young children to support, he joined the men's furnishings and sportswear departments at the store in the Bellevue Square shopping mall, across Lake Washington from Seattle. (At that point, Nordstrom had been selling men's wear for only three years.)

Nordstrom then, as now, provided little in the way of formal sales training. After teaching new employees how the cash register worked, Nordstrom dispatched them to the sales floor to learn about the merchandise and start selling. Although they were paid an hourly wage, the real money (and the scorecard for career advancement) was in high sales commissions. "I immediately saw that sales were pretty important to these guys. So, that was what I was going to give them," McCarthy recalled, with a touch of understatement. Unfortunately, he was ill-prepared for the job. "I made every mistake in the book. Although I liked to dress well, I knew virtually nothing about clothing and had no personal style. I wore my shirts too big. I didn't know how to fold garments for display or to coordinate colors and textures. Worse, because I had some learning disabilities, including dyslexia, my work habits and organizational skills were poor. I couldn't even get to work on time." After three days on the job, McCarthy's sales-per-hour track record (the company's standard of performance) was near the bottom of his department and he was told that if his performance didn't improve, he was on his way out the door.

McCarthy realized that he needed a mentor to teach him how to survive at Nordstrom. He found his role model in a co-worker named Ray Black, who was a professional men's wear salesman. Thoroughly knowledgeable about the merchandise, Black could take a swatch from a bolt of fabric that was going to be tailored for a suit and coordinate a complete wardrobe of shirts and ties, all the way down to the cufflinks. Before joining Nordstrom, Black had worked for many years in several of downtown Seattle's fine specialty men's wear shops, and his loyal clients followed him from store to store. "They came into the department asking for Ray because he identified their needs and knew how to satisfy them," said McCarthy. "Men saw him as an ally. They heeded his advice on where to get a good haircut or what style of glasses to wear. He offered them choices and suggestions and gave them the confidence to try something different. Their wives saw Ray as the mediator who could interpret their views to their husbands." McCarthy also noticed that Black had the ability to not only remember a customer's name, but his last purchase as well. "I thought to myself, 'I want to be able to do that.'" So, McCarthy volunteered to help Black whenever and wherever Black needed him, and the veteran salesman accepted the offer. "Pretty soon, we developed a routine: After Ray sold suits and sport coats to his customers, I helped them with their shirts and ties. With that increased customer contact, I was able to develop my poise and improve my interviewing skills."

Most importantly, Black taught McCarthy how to become an entrepreneur who could create his own business.

Black didn't sit around waiting for people to walk into the men's wear department; he was calling customers on the phone to alert them to new merchandise that was arriving in the store. "Ray showed me what a good salesman should be; he showed me that the Nordstrom system worked and that I could make as much money as I wanted. The way I saw it, the Nordstroms were taking all of the risks and providing all of the ingredients—the nice stores, the ambiance, the high-quality merchandise—to make it work. All I had to do was arrive every morning prepared to give an honest day's work, and to value and honor the customer."

Six months after almost being fired, Pat Kennedy, the department manager who had given McCarthy his reprieve (and who today is one of Nordstrom's top corporate footwear merchandisers), invited McCarthy to become his assistant manager in the men's wear department in a new store that Nordstrom was opening in Yakima, Washington, about 120 miles east of Seattle. McCarthy accepted the offer because it was an opportunity to help create an operation and watch it grow. (Nordstrom had already been operating a shoe store there for several years.) Yakima, which had a small middle-class population (Nordstrom's primary market), would be his litmus test.

Business was good on the Friday the Yakima store opened and continued on a respectable pace throughout the rest of weekend, but by Monday the customers had stopped coming in. "At the end of the day, Pat Kennedy and I found ourselves leaning on the balcony overlooking the selling floor, watching the cosmetic saleswomen put their merchandise away and wondering what we were going to do," McCarthy recalled. "We each had a family to support, and Nordstrom didn't pay us much in those days." They took matters into their own hands. To generate traffic, McCarthy and Kennedy turned to one of the most basic

tools for generating sales: cold calls. The two Pats and
their wives, Gretchen McCarthy and Judy Kennedy, each
seized a telephone book and a telephone and proceeded to
call the area's doctors, attorneys, automobile dealers, bank
presidents, and anyone else who might be in the market
for a nice suit.

"Whenever we got a positive reception, we sprang into
action," said McCarthy. "Whatever our customers wanted,
we obliged. We met them at their office for special fittings.
We visited their homes to help them take an inventory of
their wardrobe. We told them what to keep and what to
discard. Their wives were so appreciative, they would tell
us, 'I've been trying to tell him to get rid of that double-
knit suit for five years.' We'd start them out with the basics—traditional grey flannel suit and navy blazer, a
couple of white shirts, a couple of blue shirts, and maybe
a pinstripe. We'd finish off the wardrobe with rep ties, ar-
gyle socks, a reversible belt, and a pair of tassel loafers."

His Yakima experience represented McCarthy's first
real steps toward becoming a super salesperson. He
began developing his first personal customer book, a
looseleaf notebook that included every customer's name,
telephone number, charge account number, sizes, previous purchases, vendor preferences, likes and dislikes,
special orders, and any other characteristics, such as
being a difficult fit or preferring to shop during sales
events. He developed the habit of calling specific customers whenever special merchandise came into the
store. When birthdays or anniversaries were coming up,
he phoned his customers' wives or children with potential gift suggestions.

After four months in Yakima, McCarthy tried his hand
at being a department manager in another Nordstrom
store. But after about a year and a half, he discovered

that management wasn't for him because it took him away from sales, while sales took him away from managing. He decided to devote himself exclusively to sales, although, initially, the decision was a blow to his ego because a part of him still coveted the status and cachet of the title of department manager. "And after all, doesn't society teach us that management is the ultimate goal?" said McCarthy. "To be 'just a salesperson' doesn't sound quite enough, does it? But it was for me. The farther I got away from my management responsibilities, the more I realized that I made the right decision. Sales was what I was good at and felt comfortable with. I was, in the words of the philosopher Joseph Campbell, 'finding my bliss.'" But even when he reached a point where he felt comfortable as "just a salesperson," McCarthy's sales-education process had barely begun. Despite his extensive experience and the lessons he had learned, it wasn't until he had worked for Nordstrom for *seven* years that, in his own assessment, his skills "finally came together and my business really started to take off."

Today, McCarthy carries on the tradition of his mentor, Ray Black. Not only is McCarthy famous for his ability to remember names, sizes, and preferences, but also for his empathy, because sometimes his professional relationships with customers can progress to the profoundly personal. McCarthy, who lost his thirteen-year-old son in a fatal accident, is a sympathetic listener, whether counseling a customer whose child needs help kicking a drug habit or advising another customer on what to do with his life after retirement. "This job is more than selling clothes," he said. "It's important for me to give back to the bucket of life."

Among successful Nordstrom people, such a selfless attitude is more the rule than the exception. Whenever

Jammie Baugh, executive vice-president of Nordstrom's Southern California region, is asked to comment on Nordstrom's service, she replies, "Don't ask me. If you want to know what we're about, come in and shop our stores and talk to our people. They're the ones who can tell you." That's exactly what the authors of this book have done.

1 America's #1 Customer Service Company

A couple of dozen well-groomed and neatly dressed men and women are seated behind a horseshoe configuration of gray tables in a downtown Seattle office building near the Pike Place Market. They are a racially diverse group; most are under the age of thirty, some closer to twenty. What they have in common is that they are all new employees of Nordstrom, whose 245,000-square-foot flagship store is a few blocks from here. Awaiting the start of the one-day employee orientation that kicks off their career at the fashion specialty retail chain, some of them pick up the five-inch by eight-inch gray card in front of them—the Nordstrom Employee Handbook—and read:

WELCOME TO NORDSTROM

We're glad to have you with
our Company.
Our number one goal is to provide
outstanding customer service.
Set both your personal and
professional goals high.

We have great confidence in your
ability to achieve them.
Nordstrom Rules:
Rule #1: Use your good
judgment in all situations.
There will be no additional rules.
Please feel free to ask
your department manager,
store manager, or division general
manager any question
at any time.

For some of these men and women, this day marks the birth of a long-term relationship that will bring them financial rewards and professional and personal fulfillment. For others, it is the beginning of the end. They will eventually leave Nordstrom because of what they will perceive as unreasonable demands; persistent pressure to reach a ceaseless series of sales goals; and relentless priority on providing the kind of all-encompassing customer service—*to do virtually whatever it takes to satisfy the customer*—that has nourished the Nordstrom mystique. But the future is for later. On this orientation day, these men and women are here to immerse themselves in that very mystique and culture.

They don't realize it, but virtually everything they need to know about the secrets of Nordstrom's success can be found on the bland beige walls of this room.

One wall represents history, with a grainy, ninety-year-old picture of the original founders and partners, Carl F. Wallin and John W. Nordstrom, proudly standing outside their first tiny shoe store, Wallin & Nordstrom, in downtown Seattle; and another shot, circa 1910, of the interior of the store, where moustachioed salesmen in rumpled suits are dwarfed by stacks and stacks of shoe boxes that are stuffed along the walls and piled high up to the ceiling. There's a picture from the 1950s of John W., seated at a desk with his successors, sons Everett, Elmer, and Lloyd, admiring an "ankle-topper," a lace-up patent leather woman's shoe that retailed at the turn-of-the-century for one dollar and fifty cents.

At the opposite end of the room, functioning as a counterpoint, are individual formal portraits of the four current co-chairmen: Bruce Nordstrom, Everett's son; Elmer's sons John and James; and John "Jack" McMillan, husband of Lloyd's daughter, Loyal. Displayed on the back wall are photographs of the company's other officers, including the two co-presidents, Raymond A. Johnson and John J. Whitacre, who represent the ultimate in career advancement for non-family members. Johnson joined Nordstrom in 1969 and rose through the ranks as a store manager and regional general manager and vice-president. Whitacre began working for Nordstrom in 1976. He had been a buyer, merchandise manager, store manager, and regional general manager and vice-president. Both were named co-president in 1992.

Dispersed around the room are several three-foot by two-foot placards that feature head shots of outstanding employees and details of their career paths up the Nordstrom "Pyramid of Success" to the position of store manager. Typical of these employees is Kari Scanlan, who in 1981 started as a "rover" [a sales associate not assigned to one particular department] in the suburban Seattle Bellevue Square store, advanced through a series of buying and managing positions in Washington state and California. Today, she is a buyer in Nordstrom's Direct Sales (catalog) Division.

Another woman, K.C. Shaffer, who was at the time manager of the downtown Seattle store (and is currently a corporate merchandiser), summed up the quintessential

Nordstrom "can-do" spirit with this quote that was printed on her placard: "At age ten, my goal was to work for Nordstrom and after selling at Town Square from 1973 to 1976, my goal was to be the downtown store manager. My future goal is to be a general manager, and I am grateful for the opportunity to work at Nordstrom."

Goal setting, as these new associates will soon learn, fuels the Nordstrom engine. Therefore, in another part of the room, there is a list of individual annual goals for net sales (total sales minus returns) that associates must meet or exceed in order to attain the elite rank of "Pacesetter." (Pacesetter targets vary with each department. In men's shoes, it's $410,000; in women's apparel, it's $385,000.)

Bruce Parker, the energetic training coordinator who is leading today's orientation, stands at the front of the room, dressed in a white shirt, patterned tie, and pleated slacks. After introducing himself to the new associates and checking attendance, Parker then instructs them to "Introduce yourself to the person next to you. Find out their name, where they are from, what their job is going to be here at Nordstrom, and something interesting about them. Not just 'I'm married and have two kids, we live in a rambler house and drive a station wagon.' We want to know something *really* interesting; something *exciting;* maybe you're an ex-Olympic athlete or you dance with the Pacific Northwest Ballet on your time off. Move around the room; meet somebody brand new. I'll give you four minutes."

Parker's instructions set off a buzz of animated conversation, even some genuine laughter, that lasts until he brings the room to order and calls on a couple of people to start things off by introducing to the group the person they've just met.

"This is Jackie," says a blonde woman dressed in a turtleneck sweater, stirrup pants, and blazer. "She works at the Tacoma store in the Cafe. And she enjoys tap dancing."

"Tap dancing, huh?," says Parker good-naturedly. "If we get bored, you can do some tap dancing for us. Welcome."

"This is Connie," says Jackie, an Asian-American woman with short black hair, who wears a short-sleeved blouse and pleated slacks. "She works at the Alderwood Mall store in the Brass Plum (Junior Sportswear) department as a stocker. One of the things she likes about Nordstrom is that her brother worked at the Northgate store and got on with the company without having a high school diploma. It was exciting for her to see how the company stood behind him and promoted him, encouraged him to go to school, and gave him a lot of wonderful opportunities."

And so it goes around the room. Not all are in sales. One man, an immigrant from Haiti, is a tax accountant in the payroll department; a woman who spent five years as a cook on an Alaska fishing boat now works in Nordstrom's catering division.

Parker then plays a word association game, asking them what comes to mind when they hear the term "customer service." The answers come firing back to the training leader, who quickly jots them down on a blackboard:

"Product knowledge."

"Courtesy."

"Smiles."

"Solution-oriented."

"Follow through."

"Coordination."

"Professionalism."

"Find a need and fill it."

"Don't make promises you can't keep."

"Pleasing your customer."

Sounds simple enough, doesn't it? Nordstrom's initial message to new hires probably doesn't differ very much from thousands of other companies: Take care of the customer; do your job; blah, blah, blah. But what sets Nordstrom apart is that it translates these pronouncements into performance; it converts precepts into profits.

■ The Nordstrom Mystique

At a time when "customer service" is the buzzword of American business, Nordstrom has become the standard against which other companies privately, and sometimes publicly, measure themselves. Nordstrom is invariably cited by consultants, business school educators, and authors of customer service books as "the universal ambition of retailing," in the words of one retail columnist. Peter Glen, the customer service guru and author of *It's Not My Department,* says the Nordstrom shopping experience "can bring tears of joy to the eyes of customers." On his first trip to Seattle, Paul Smith, who was then North American director for Brooks Brothers' parent company, Marks and Spencer, told the *Seattle Times* in 1992 that when he first arrived in Seattle, he "made a beeline for Nordstrom. . . . I think they have a lot to teach the rest of us in the realm of service." The *New Yorker,* which covered the opening day of the new store at the Garden State Plaza in Paramus, New Jersey, in 1991, described Nordstrom as a chain "that makes retailing an event rather than just retailing." After Nordstrom opened its first midwestern store in suburban Chicago in 1991, commentator Paul Harvey told his national radio audience, "This store is teaching its eastern neighbors some manners." Harvey said he visited Nordstrom's Oak Brook Mall store three times in the first three days it was open and on "the third day I bought stock in the company." The Nordstrom mystique occasionally assumes mythic stature. A profile of the company in the *New York Times Magazine* quoted a Bel Air, California, minister who delivered a sermon entitled "The Gospel According to Nordstrom." The minister praised the retailer "for carrying out the call of the gospel in ways more consistent and caring than we sometimes do in the church."

The most sincere form of flattery is the response of the competition. When Nordstrom invaded California in the late seventies, "They changed the face of retailing," Frank Arnone, then chairman of the Broadway department store told *Women's Wear Daily (WWD)*. "For the customers willing to pay full price, they were the retailer of choice because of service and assortment. Los Angeles once had a reputation for having the most disinterested sales help in the United States, but that began to change with the arrival of Nordstrom." An executive from the Bullock's department store chain told *WWD* that before Nordstrom, retailers "had kind of lost track of the customer. Everybody was out just trying to sell things." Soon after Nordstrom opened a mammoth 330,000-square-foot store in downtown San Francisco, a man purchased a dress shirt at the Emporium, a rival retailer adjacent to Nordstrom on Market Street. As he headed toward the exit, the sales clerk suddenly called out to him and asked him to stop. The puzzled customer wondered what the trouble was. "Can I have your package back?" pleaded the clerk. When the customer handed it over, the clerk reached into the bag, fished out the sales slip and scribbled a quick "thank-you" on it. "Ever since Nordstrom came to San Francisco," he lamented, "we have to do that."

Pursuit of the Nordstrom ideal is not limited to retailers. Bob Middlemas, general manager of Nordstrom's Midwest region, once received a phone call from a principal of an elementary school in Chicago, asking him to provide her with some information about the Nordstrom philosophy because she wanted her school to become the "Nordstrom of education." The Capitol Hill newspaper *Roll Call* once ran an article about certain politicians' success in being able to make the political TV talk shows their own personal vehicles. One of *Roll Call*'s can't-miss tips for getting booked on those shows: "Have a press representative who takes the Nordstrom approach." A senior vice-president of Equifax, the credit-reporting company, once promised that he would have his employees "thinking like Nordstrom," with customer service as their guiding principle. A trade publication for the National Association of Home Builders recommended that builders examine Nordstrom's service policies as one way to attract home buyers in a buyers' market. In particular, the publication cited the way Nordstrom's salespeople take the time to learn about their customers' lifestyles and needs and then adapt inventories in their stores to local tastes. The publication recommended that home builders visit potential buyers "in their current homes to see how they live."

In a November 1993 column about achieving excellence in the workplace, Tom Peters wrote:

> Suppose you commit to new heights in quality or service here and now. In your own mind, you're an instant Nordstrom (retail) or Motorola (manufacturing). But your next task—dratted real world!—is to go through your boring in-basket. What an opportunity! So you don't know

much about Nordstrom or Motorola; nonetheless, respond to the first item in your in-basket as you imagine a Nordstrom or Motorola exec would. A memo from a front-line worker complaining about a silly roadblock to improvement? An irate note from a customer or distributor. "Nordstrom" it. . . . Act it out, in a small way, your Nordstrom-Motorola fantasy of matchless quality.

What makes Nordstrom so unique? The chain is geared toward middle-to-upper-income women and men. It offers these customers attractive stores with a large, varied, and competitively priced inventory of shoes, apparel, accessories, and cosmetics and a liberal return policy. But a lot of stores do that. What separates Nordstrom from its competitors is its army of highly motivated, "self-empowered people who have an entrepreneurial spirit, who feel that they're in this to better themselves and to feel good about themselves, to make more money and to be successful," Bruce Nordstrom told Morley Safer on a 1990 *60 Minutes* feature entitled "The Nordstrom Boys."

These sales people have the opportunity to be successful because *Nordstrom gives its employees the freedom to make decisions. And Nordstrom management is willing to live with those decisions.*

Everything else flows from that premise. Because Nordstrom has the faith and trust in its frontline people to push decision-making responsibilities down to the sales floor, the Nordstrom shopping experience is "as close to working with the owner of a small business as a customer can get," said Harry Mullikin, chairman emeritus of Westin Hotels. Nordstrom salespeople "can make any decision that needs to be made. It's like dealing with a one-person shop."

Donald E. Petersen, the retired chairman of the Ford Motor Company and a longtime student of customer service and total quality management, believes the key to Nordstrom's success is that "Nordstrom gives all of their employees the charge to service the customer and the authority to do it. The evidence is clear. You look like a far better manager and supervisor when you give power to people, because it energizes them; you get their ideas and not just your own, so you have a much broader base of ideas from which to draw when you are making decisions." In 1981, when he headed Ford, Petersen sought the consultation of W. Edwards Deming, the famed expert on business management who advised the Japanese on how to rebuild their industry after World War II. Deming, who died in 1993 at the age of ninety-three, spent the last years of his life encouraging American corporations such as Ford and Xerox to consider workers as *partners* rather than *antagonists*. In order to do that, these corporations had to transform their entire culture.

As the idea of "empowering the workers" has become the new mantra of business, the basic question facing American industry is this: *Why have so few companies been willing to implement this simple concept?*

"I've been puzzling over that since 1981, when I met Ed Deming," said Petersen, who finally came to the conclusion that management, "is afraid to give frontline employees the power and authority to make a difference. They are afraid that someone will screw up, which will make them look bad.

"We all know that mistakes will be made, and that every now and then there will be a bad apple. But that shouldn't deter a company from following a process of continuing to improve how it functions. The leadership has to make it clear that [empowering workers] is part of the ethic and approach of the organization. Deming said that customers would get better products and services when workers were encouraged to use their minds—as well as their hands—on the job. At Ford, it was wonderful to watch how energized people become when you empower them. It became obvious to me, as I got more acquainted with the Nordstrom stores, that this was their magic. Until another store gets brave enough to go as far as Nordstrom does in that respect, I say there is no one that equals the Nordstrom approach to serving the customer."

Jammie Baugh, executive vice-president and general manager of Nordstrom's Southern California region, who has worked for the company for two decades, said, "Giving away responsibility and authority is the ultimate expression of leadership. At Nordstrom, we create an environment for empowerment. We assemble a team and allow them to fail, but obviously, we're there for them when they need us." Baugh recalled a rival retailer once telling her, "We don't want the inmates to run the asylum." Baugh replied, "That's funny, at Nordstrom, we *do* want the inmates to run the asylum."

Nordstrom expects, encourages, preaches, and demands individual initiative from the people who are on the front lines, people who have the freedom to generate their own ideas (rather than wait for an edict from above) and to promote fashion directions that are representative of their store and region. The best Nordstrom sales associates will do virtually everything they can to make sure a shopper leaves the store a satisfied customer, carrying home *the right item in the right size in the right color at the right price.* To make it easier for the sales associates to make sales, Nordstrom stocks a large range of sizes. "There's no sense even having a style unless you have a pair in every size, because the minute I miss the customer's size, she doesn't care how many pairs I've got," said co-chairman John Nordstrom. "That's how you run a retail business." Consequently, Nordstrom demands that shoe companies stock and restock the sizes Nordstrom needs. Nevertheless, most shoe companies are understandably reluctant to carry large, costly inventories; they'd rather offer pre-packed cases of the most popular sizes. "But 50 percent of the people don't wear those sizes," Bruce Nordstrom claimed. "One of the aspects of our reputation is that we appeal to everyone." If customers complain that the store is out of their shoe size or a salesperson didn't measure both of their feet, Nordstrom reacts. "When the customer talks, we jump," is a popular Nordstromism.

Tom Peters once wrote about a man who sent a letter to Nordstrom that described his difficulty in getting a suit he bought there to fit—despite several visits for alterations. When the letter reached John Nordstrom's desk, he sent over a new suit to the customer's office, along with a Nordstrom tailor to make sure the jacket and pants were perfect. When alterations were completed, the suit was delivered at no charge.

The most motivated employees perform "heroics," which are the kind of above-and-beyond-the-call-of-duty acts of customer service that are embedded in the Nordstrom mystique. There is the story of a customer who fell in love with a pair of burgundy, pleated Donna Karan slacks that had just gone on sale at the Nordstrom store in downtown Seattle. But the store was out of her size and the sales associate was unable to track down a pair at the five other Nordstrom stores in the Seattle area. Aware that the same slacks were available across the street at a competitor, the associate secured some petty cash from her department manager, marched across the street to the Frederick and Nelson department store, where she bought the slacks (at full price), returned to Nordstrom, and then sold them to the customer for the marked-down Nordstrom price. Obviously, Nordstrom didn't make money on that sale, but it was an investment in promoting the loyalty of an appreciative customer, who, more than likely, thought of Nordstrom for her next purchase.

Some legitimate "heroic" stories sound apocryphal. Perhaps the most famous one—which the national press frequently cites—is the tale of the salesperson who gladly took back a set of automobile tires and gave the customer a refund. Nordstrom has never sold tires, but the story is true. In 1975, Nordstrom acquired three stores in Alaska from the Northern Commercial Company, which did sell tires. So, when the customer—who had purchased the tires from Northern Commercial—brought them back to Nordstrom, the return was accepted. Nevertheless, the hyperbole reinforces the point and nurtures the mythology.

"Those [heroic] stories are . . . tales of convenience, hassle-free buying, and saved time," wrote Edward H. Meyer in *Direct Marketing Magazine.* "The thing that makes Nordstrom's emphasis on service so appealing is not the fuzzy warmth of personal pampering. [Customers] go there because terrific service makes Nordstrom so incredibly convenient. Nordstrom helps consumers save time." (Examples of how Nordstrom salespeople save time will be explained in greater detail in later chapters.)

Nordstrom customers are incredibly loyal. They may move to an area where there is no Nordstrom, but that doesn't mean that their relationship with Nordstrom is over. Take, for example, Jerry Grinstein, chairman and chief executive officer of Burlington Northern Railroad, a former Seattleite, who said, "We live in Dallas, Texas, where there is no Nordstrom. So, whenever we are in a city that has a Nordstrom, that's where we do our shopping." [A new Nordstrom store is scheduled to open in Dallas in 1996.]

In the early 1990s, when the residents of Santa Clarita, a suburb north of Los Angeles, were polled on what improvements they would like to see in their community, the number-one answer was to have their own Nordstrom store.

Nordstrom, which by the end of 1995 had fifty-nine full-line stores and seventeen clearance stores in twelve states, generates annual sales of almost $4 billion, of which 38 percent is women's apparel, 20 percent women's accessories, 20 percent shoes, 16 percent men's apparel and furnishings, 4 percent children's apparel and accessories, and 2 percent miscellaneous merchandise. (Nordstrom also operates leased shoe departments in eleven Liberty House department stores in Hawaii.) Nordstrom boasts a sales-per-square-foot performance of $400, which is almost double the industry average. "We're great believers in high sales-per-square-foot," said co-chairman Bruce Nordstrom. "We don't know how to run a business with modest per-square-foot sales."

The company is generally acknowledged to be the first apparel retailer in the country to pay sales commissions as a performance incentive. (Nordstrom has been awarding commission on footwear for many decades.) Sales associates average the highest pay in the retail apparel industry—$24,000 a year; some make in excess of $50,000, and a few earn more than $100,000. With Nordstrom's profit-sharing plan (which will be explained in Chapter 4), employees can potentially add tens of thousands of dollars in annual personal income; some can retire or leave the company with several hundred thousand dollars—before the age of fifty.

But Nordstrom is not perfect. The urgency to compete and perform is ferocious, so working for this company is not for the fainthearted. In a blistering, 1990 front-page article in *The Wall Street Journal,* staff reporter Susan C. Faludi wrote of Nordstrom employees who couldn't take "an environment of constant pressure and harassment that incites employees to prey on each other." An attorney for Local 1001 and Local 37 of the Union of Food and Commercial Workers (which at the time represented workers at the six Seattle-Tacoma area Nordstrom stores) told *60 Minutes* that "the working conditions of the 1920s are alive and well at Nordstrom." For three years, the company was engaged in a rancorous, highly publicized battle with Locals 1001 and 37. The battle began in 1989 when Nordstrom and the union were negotiating a new three-year contract. The most contentious issue was a request by some employees to make Nordstrom an open shop, which meant that union membership would be optional. (The six Nordstrom Seattle-area stores had been closed shops for many years.) When the union refused to put that choice to a vote of the members, the contract talks hit an impasse. Fighting for its life, the union filed a class action lawsuit against Nordstrom, claiming that some employees were not equitably reimbursed under minimum-wage laws for "off-the-clock" work such as attending store meetings, writing thank-you notes, and delivering merchandise to customers. Finally, in a 1993 out-of-court agreement, Nordstrom agreed that about 31,000 current and former employees might be eligible for back pay and set aside a reserve of about $15 million. However, not all 31,000 employees filed claims for back pay, and of those who did, not all proved to be eligible, so that far less than the $15 million reserve was used. [This complex episode, which was Nordstrom's first major public black eye, is explored in greater depth in Chapter 6.]

Despite the union's victories, the locals were decertified in 1992 by a vote of Nordstrom sales associates because they did not "express the desires of the Nordstrom employees in Seattle; they [had] their own agenda, which [was] not in our best interest," said Joe Dover, who has sold shoes at the Bellevue Square (Washington) store for more than a decade, and who was one of the leaders in the fight to decertify the union. "Demands and expectations are high, but if you like working in an unrestricted environment, it's a great place to work. They provide you with great merchandise and the freedom to do what you want."

Van Mensah, who sells men's clothes in the suburban Washington, D.C., Pentagon City store, always advises prospective Nordstrom employees, "if you're interested in retail, this is the best place to work. But you have to understand that this is not for everybody."

Martha S. Wikstrom, vice-president and general manager of Nordstrom's Capital region, echoed that thought: "People who don't want to sell will never make it in our system because if you don't understand how important that is, and if you don't understand how important the relationship with the customer is, you just won't do well here."

An outsider's perspective comes from Jerry Miller, president of Shoe Biz, a New York footwear manufacturer, who wrote in his 1984 book, *The Wandering Shoe,* that "Nordstrom develops the character of its people. You start at the bottom and do it the Nordstrom way, and those standards are unnegotiable. It comes right from the top. They are high-grade people. It is a company that builds and develops character, and if you start at the bottom and survive the various steps and move you develop into one hell of a man [or woman]."

■ A Family Business

Back at the employee orientation, the new hires watch a twelve-minute video, "The Nordstrom Story," which includes a brief history of the company and interviews with Elmer (the last surviving brother, who died in 1993), Bruce, John, and Jim Nordstrom that help to personalize and humanize the company. After the video is over, a tall, blond-haired man enters the room, walking to the front to address the new employees. He is Blake Nordstrom, Bruce's son, who is vice-president and general manager of the Washington state and Alaska group of stores, and one of several Nordstrom scions (all in their late twenties or early thirties) who represent the fourth generation of the family. Blake first began working in the store at the age of ten, sweeping floors in the downtown shoe stockroom. At thirteen, he stocked shoes; at fifteen, he began selling shoes and from then on he worked for the company while attending the University of Washington. After graduation, he served as a buyer, merchandiser, department manager, and store manager in company stores around the country. Standing about six feet two inches tall, with the close-cropped haircut of a college basketball player, Blake speaks in a quiet, unassuming voice. "I like to come to these meetings and meet people. My name is Blake and I'm really excited to have you here." The first thing he tells the new employees is that "there's nothing new" in customer service. "We are fond of saying that the best training you can have is your parents. Did they teach you to be nice, and smile and work hard? If you have those qualities, you can sell lots of stuff and you'll succeed in our company. We're all in this together. It's in my best interest to help each of you succeed. If you do well, then I'll do well."

With the Nordstrom family holding the largest single portion of the stock of this publicly traded company, the continuity of family management is one of the most important reasons for Nordstrom's success. Family is a metaphor that permeates the Nordstrom culture. Back in the days when they ran the company, Elmer, Lloyd, and Everett put on annual summer picnics for employees and their spouses and children at the family's summer place on Hood Canal on Washington state's Olympic Peninsula, and gave Christmas dinner dance parties at Seattle's stately

Olympic Hotel. "Some companies demand loyalty from personnel, but we felt that loyalty should come from us to them, first," said Elmer. "Loyalty is something earned, not expected." The Nordstrom brothers' sons have carried on this tradition. In 1994, when the Juvenile Diabetes Foundation wanted to present its "Man of the Year" award to the Nordstroms, the Nordstroms insisted that the award be given to the "Nordstrom Family," including everybody from "blood brother to sales associate," in Bruce Nordstrom's words.

Although they are shy with the media, when it comes to employees and customers, the Nordstroms are approachable and accessible. They rarely close the doors of their offices (the company's employee newsletter is called "The Open Door") and all of them answer their own phones. If they are not immediately available, they will return phone calls. Tom Peters used to mention this trait at his seminars. In fact, during a lunch break at one of those seminars, one of the attendees decided to see if it was really true. After the lunch break, the man interrupted Peters's lecture to tell Peters and the audience that he had, in fact, just called Bruce Nordstrom. Bruce wasn't in his office but the call was patched through to him on the sales floor, and they had a conversation for fifteen minutes.

Betsy Sanders, a former Nordstrom executive who is now a retail consultant and a member of the board of directors of Wal-Mart Stores, remembered the day in 1974 when she was managing the Town Square women's apparel department in a Nordstrom store north of Seattle, and she saw all of the Nordstroms coming through the store on their way to a meeting about some real estate matters. She noticed that Bruce had a look of consternation on his face. He motioned towards Sanders and pointed to two women who were leaving the store, complaining that "they were never so disappointed in their lives." Bruce asked Sanders to find out what had happened.

"Bruce went off to his meeting and I went off to stop these women," Sanders recalled. "I explained that Mr. Nordstrom had overheard what they had said and was very worried that we had disappointed them. They started to laugh. They said, 'We wish you could do something for us. We've got champagne tastes but a beer income.' They had fallen in love with a dress in the Gallery Department, but they couldn't afford it. I said I might be able to help them." Sanders brought them over to her more moderately priced department and eventually sold them each two dresses, which cost less than the one dress that had first admired. "I had been at Nordstrom for three years and I thought, 'Wow, this is what Nordstrom is all about.' It's about the chief executive officer going to an important real estate meeting and yet still caring most about what was happening on the floor," said Sanders.

But that's not the end of the story. Several hours later, the Nordstroms came out of their meeting, "looking bedraggled," Sanders continued. "Bruce came over to me and said, 'Betsy, I know you took care of those customers. I just want to hear what the story was.' That was just emblazoned on me. I thought, 'My gosh, the customer *is* number one with them. It doesn't matter what's on his mind. He's not going to forget there is a customer with a need.'" That's the Nordstrom difference.

A Seattle journalist once compared the Nordstrom family to Mount Rainier, the 14,410-foot peak that towers over the Cascade Range of Washington state. "As the mountain symbolizes the beauty and splendor of the Northwest," wrote Fred Moody in *Seattle Weekly,* "so the Nordstrom name has come to epitomize a certain Northwestness of character, a set of drives and values that we regard as being unique to our corner of the country."

The story of how Nordstrom got to be that way, how it has produced an entrepreneurial culture that, despite its flaws, is admired by corporations throughout this country, starts with a Swedish immigrant and his sons, who created the atmosphere of hard work and competition that remains the hallmark of this quintessentially Pacific Northwest company.

KEYS TO SUCCESS

Nordstrom is the customer service standard against which other companies measure themselves. Nordstrom is invariably cited by consultants, business school educators, and authors of customer service books as the universal ambition of retailing. What separates Nordstrom from its competitors is its army of motivated, self-empowered entrepreneurial men and women.

Nordstrom is successful because of the following principles:

- Nordstrom empowers its employees with the freedom to make decisions, and is willing to live with those decisions. Delegating authority and accountability is the ultimate expression of leadership.
- Nordstrom expects, encourages, preaches, and demands individual initiative and ideas from its front-line people.
- Because Nordstrom pushes decision-making responsibilities down to the sales floor, shopping with a Nordstrom salesperson is like working with the owner of a small business.
- Nordstrom's best salespeople will do virtually everything possible to ensure that a shopper leaves the store a satisfied customer.
- Full inventories are a measure of customer service. To make it easier for employees to make sales, Nordstrom stocks a wide and deep range of sizes, so that there is something for virtually everyone.
- Motivated employees perform "heroics"—acts of outstanding customer service, which are part of the Nordstrom mystique.
- Working at Nordstrom is not for everybody. Demands and expectations are high. The people who succeed enjoy working in an unrestricted environment.

After the Gold Rush

A Store Is Born

Johan W. Nordstrom, like the founders of most of America's retail dynasties, was an immigrant, and was driven by the immigrant's intense desire to succeed. The middle child of five, Johan was born February 15, 1871, in the town of Alvik Neder Lulea, in the northernmost part of Sweden, sixty miles below the Arctic Circle. His father, who was a blacksmith, wagon maker, and part-time farmer, passed away when Johan was eight years old. By the time he was eleven, his mother had taken him out of school to put him to work on the family farm. His life in Sweden, by Johan's own admission, was an unhappy one. Although he was just a young teenager, his mother "seemed to think I was a man, and often remarked that at my age, my brother [ten years his senior] could do nearly anything and why couldn't I," he wrote in a privately published memoir. "I often cried when I had trouble doing things she expected me to do and couldn't, and felt very helpless."

Because the farm was too small to share with his older brother, Johan left Sweden the winter he turned sixteen. With 450 crowns (about $112) of his modest inheritance, he bought a suit, "the first clothes I had ever had on my back that were not homespun and hand-woven." His eventual destination was the Pacific Northwest of America, where thousands of Swedes thrived as fishermen, loggers, blacksmiths, shipwrights, and millwrights in a climate and landscape similar to their homeland. Others helped finish the transcontinental railroads. "Give me enough Swedes," proclaimed James J. Hill, the creator of the Great Northern Railroad, "and I'll build a railroad right through hell."

There were no railroads in northern Sweden, so Johan and two young friends began their odyssey to America with a two-day boat trip to Stockholm. From there, they traveled another three days by boat, through the Gota Canal, to Gothenburg, then sailed to Hull, England. The first train ride of Johan's life brought him to Liverpool, where he took steerage passage for the ten-day voyage to Ellis Island, New York. From there, Nordstrom and his friends, barely able to speak a word of English, took a train to Stambaugh, Michigan, where he had a cousin who told him of prospects for work. With five dollars in his pocket, he took a job carting and loading iron ore onto railroad cars, for which he was paid $1.60 for a ten-hour day. (He nearly lost his life in an iron ore slide.) For the next five years, his strong back and unrelenting determination carried him westward through a series of hardscrabble manual labors: logging in Michigan, coal-digging in Iowa, gold and silver mining in Colorado, loading railroad ties and carting brick in Mendocino County, California, and logging redwood trees in California and Douglas fir trees in Washington. By the summer of 1896, Nordstrom had saved enough money to buy twenty acres of bottom land for potato farming in the Swedish immigrant enclave of Arlington, Washington, about fifty miles north of Seattle.

■ Seattle: City of Opportunity

Seattle in the 1890s was "young, raw, and crude," wrote Roger Sale in *Seattle, Past to Present*. White settlers first reached the region in 1852, and it wasn't until 1860 that a group of about 150 pioneers settled there. (By way of comparison, New York City in the 1850s already had paved streets and a store named R.H. Macy.) "They didn't come looking for paradise," said one wag. "They came for the cheap real estate." From 1879 to 1890, population rocketed from 1,107 to 43,487, fueled by constant rumors that Seattle would be the terminus of the transcontinental railroad. The nascent city provided equal opportunity for God-fearing pioneers, entrepreneurial visionaries, scam artists, and ladies of the evening. The essence of the "Seattle Spirit" was "enlightened self-interest," wrote William C. Speidel, the city's iconoclastic historian, in his irreverent account, *Sons of the Profits.*

When Nordstrom passed through on his way to Arlington, the city of Seattle was still rebuilding itself from the ruins of 1889's great fire, which destroyed virtually all of the sixty-four-acre downtown core and left $10 million in damages. But rather than cramping the city's growth, the fire actually ignited it. Population increased in the year after the disaster from 38,000 to 43,000; many of the newcomers came to rebuild the city's unpaved streets and sewers and erect new commercial buildings and schools. There were "enough brickmakers, masons, ironworkers, foundries, electrical workers, plumbers, cement manufacturers, and roofers so that the fire was in fact a boon to an expanding and increasingly diversified economy," described author Roger Sale. Others came to speculate on real estate, following the Great Northern's selection of Seattle (instead of arch-rival Tacoma) as the end of its line.

The mood was feverish. Making money was on everyone's mind. A leading banker of that era described it
as one "of adventure and wildcat speculation . . . such as
can never again be witnessed." Norman H. Clark wrote in
Washington: A Bicentennial History: "There had been
nothing like it in the American history since the opening
of the Louisiana Territory—golden years where no personal ambition, however grandiose, seemed at all unreasonable, when it seemed that every venture might
prosper and every family might share in the nobility
of wealth because of the democracy of profit." But not everyone was so lucky. Yesler Way—the steep trail where
timber workers skidded logs down the hill to Henry
Yesler's steam sawmill on the waterfront—gave birth to
the sobriquet of broken dreams: Skid Road.

Seattle's diversified economy—forest products, coal,
salmon, and farm crops (particularly hops and wheat)—
spared the region the financial devastation caused by the
1893 worldwide financial panic, which triggered a stock
market collapse and nationwide bank failures and bank
runs. With the country faced with an undersupply of
gold for coinage and repaying foreign debts, the cash-
strapped eastern banks (which helped finance western
expansion) began calling in notes. With the money supply in the West dried up, Seattle's army of boosters, pro-
moters, charlatans, and flacks went to work, kicking off
a spirited competition with Tacoma, to become the "Gateway to the Orient," and reap the benefits of trade with
Asian countries. That dream was realized in 1896, when
the Japanese freighter *Miike Maru* arrived in Seattle,
launching the first regular shipping service between
Japan and the West Coast of the United States.

At breakfast, on the Sunday morning of July 18, 1897,
Johan Nordstrom picked up the *Seattle Post-Intelligencer*

to see splashed across the front page, in huge capital letters, the magic word: "*GOLD!*"

At long last, the rumors were true; coarse gold had been found in the fields of the Klondike, in Canada's Yukon Territory. Five thousand people greeted the steamer *Portland* when it arrived at the Seattle waterfront with a much ballyhooed cargo of "a ton of gold." Coupled with the arrival in San Francisco of the *Excelsior*, with another heavy cargo of gold, the news ignited the world. A front-page story in the following day's *San Francisco Chronicle* described the frenzy in Seattle:

> It is safe to say that never in the history of the Northwest has there been such excitement as has prevailed in this city all day long and which is raging tonight. It is due to the arrival . . . of the steamer *Portland*, carrying sixty-eight men from the Clondyke (sic) gold fields, everyone of whom brings down a fortune.
>
> There have been so many stories sent out from Alaska of great strikes which later proved to be without foundation that people were reaching that period where they refused to credit them. But when the big *Portland* ran alongside the ocean dock at eight o'clock this morning and those sixty-eight men . . . walked down the gangplank struggling to hold up the weight of gold which was stacked high on their shoulders, the thousands of people who stood on the dock to receive them were suddenly seized with Clondyke fever, and tonight Clondyke is on the lips of every man, woman, and child of this city.

In Arlington, Nordstrom and a friend were reading a similar, breathless account in the local newspaper. "Finally I slammed the paper down on the table and said, 'I'm going to Alaska; will you go with me?,'" Nordstrom recalled in his memoir. After the friend declined, Nordstrom collected his belongings and "what little money I had and by four o'clock that afternoon I was on the train bound for Seattle and a new adventure." When he reached the Seattle waterfront early the following morning, he found a virtually endless line waiting to buy a ticket for Alaska.

A week later, Nordstrom boarded the coal freighter *Willamette* with 1,200 men, 600 horses, and 600 mules. (With only a second-class passage, Nordstrom shared sleeping quarters with the mules.) Reaching Port Valdez, Alaska, in Prince William Sound, Nordstrom had just begun a thousand-mile adventure to Dawson, the frontier town in the heart of the gold fields. The real challenge lay in reaching Skagway, which had sprouted up virtually overnight as the departure point for Dawson. Getting to Skagway was a matter of trial and error because accurate information on accessible routes and reliable transportation was scanty at best; some established trails were washed out by rain or covered by mudslides, and water routes were just as unreliable. Nordstrom battled cold, snow, rain, storms, and wind—mostly on foot, because his horse died along the way and was butchered for food. From Skagway, he walked over the already frozen-solid Klondike River into the tiny town of Dawson, barely a year old, but "as lively a little place as you'd ever see," he recalled. "There were many saloons, dance halls, and gambling houses, all waiting for the poor miner to spend his hard-earned gold."

For the next two years, Nordstrom struggled in the gold fields, taking a series of odd jobs to keep going. Finally, he hit pay dirt. But before he could celebrate his good luck, his claim was challenged by another miner. Claim disputes, which were common, were settled by the Canadian gold commissioner, who happened to be the brother of Nordstrom's challenger. Fully aware that corruption was no stranger to the Yukon, Nordstrom knew that his chances of winning arbitration were slim, so he sold his share of the claim for $13,000, which, he wrote, "looked like a lot of money to me."

With cash in hand, Nordstrom returned to Seattle, a boom town propelled by a blast of new arrivals and fueled by the financial windfall of the Klondike gold rush. "There was a swagger in its walk, a boldness in its vision," a historian wrote about Seattle's mad dash toward the twentieth century. "Out here, on the edge of the continent, the great Pacific lapping at the front door, all things seemed possible." Civic boosters and hyperactive press agents, who had previously hyped the city as the "Gateway to the Orient," now ballyhooed Seattle as the "Gateway to the Yukon." Between 1898 and 1902, $174 million in gold was assayed in Seattle, much of it finding its way into the coffers of local merchants such as Frederick & Nelson and The Bon Marche, which supplied food, clothing, and equipment for the prospectors heading to the far North. Seattle's population soared, and the waterfront area moved to the rhythms of raunchy honky-tonks and flamboyant brothels flooded with red velvet.

■ The Birth of the Business

In May 1900, Nordstrom (who had since anglicized his given name to John) married Hilda Carlson, a Swedish girl he had courted before going to Alaska, and the two began looking around for a business to get into. He often visited an old Klondike pal, Carl F. Wallin, a shoemaker with a bushy walrus moustache, who owned a shoe repair shop on Fourth Avenue and Pike Street. Wallin suggested that he and Nordstrom form a partnership in a shoe store that would be established on the site of the repair shop.

Nordstrom agreed, putting up $5,000; Wallin added $1,000, and the Wallin & Nordstrom shoe store was born. Some of the money was used to fix up the store, which was immediately expanded from a ten-foot to a twenty-foot-wide front. With $3,500, they bought an inventory of shoes, retailing from $1.95 to $4.95, and opened in 1901.

Selling shoes was a rather odd venture for both men, who spoke only broken English, and wore ill-fitting, rumpled wool suits that bunched up at the knees and elbows. Nordstrom later recalled:

> I had never fitted a pair of shoes or sold anything in my life, but I was depending on Mr. Wallin's meager knowledge of shoe salesmanship to help me out. Well, this opening day we had not had a customer by noon, so my partner went to lunch. He had not been gone but a few minutes when our first customer, a woman, came in for a pair of shoes she had seen in the window. I was nervous and could not find the style she had picked out in our stock. I was just about ready to give up when I decided to try on the pair from the window, the only pair we had of that style. I'll never know if it was the right size, but the customer bought them anyway.

Opening day sales totaled $12.50. The next day, Saturday, the store stayed open from eight o'clock in the morning until midnight; receipts nearly quadrupled to $47. By the end of that first summer, Saturday sales sometimes reached as high as $100. "We both allowed ourselves a salary of $75 a month and got along fine on this amount," Nordstrom wrote. "The store was so small and looked so poor that the fellows from the better factories back East wouldn't even call on us to sell us shoes." At first, he and Wallin bought shoes by relying on the advice of traveling salesmen. Because neither man knew anything about merchandising, they simply bought shoes in all medium-size ranges. But, Nordstrom later claimed, soon they discovered that those sizes weren't large enough for their rawboned Swedish friends. That story might be apocryphal, but the fact is, Wallin & Nordstrom began carrying larger and wider sizes. This decision led to the company's establishing a national reputation for the depth and breadth of its inventory, which continues to be one of the cornerstones of customer service the Nordstrom way. Today, Nordstrom packs its selling spaces with the highest value of inventory per-square-foot of any specialty apparel retailer in the country—20 to 30 percent more than the competition.

Wallin & Nordstrom's business increased, reaching annual sales of $47,000 by 1905. Forced to move to another location, they acquired the stock and location of Berry Brothers shoe store on Second Avenue near Pike Street for $21,000. With Nordstrom putting up his two houses and some property in Seattle's Rainier Valley as collateral, the partners secured a $10,000 loan from the Scandinavian-American Bank, which helped finance the businesses of many Scandinavian entrepreneurs, including Nels Nelson, co-founder of the Frederick & Nelson department store.

Wallin & Nordstrom moved several times, expanding, updating, and upgrading their presentation. Rather than carry fashion, the partners preferred the stable, staid business of high-quality, conservative shoes, particularly corrective "health" shoes, which were very popular at the time. What the stores lacked in ambiance they made up in the inventory, which was piled on shelves stretching up to the twenty-foot-high ceiling, where they could be reached by climbing ladders equipped with wheels. Baskets were used to carry money and purchases up to the cashier on the mezzanine.

Because of the city's frontier status and isolation from the major population centers, Seattle's boosters were constantly scheming to pull off something spectacular to get the attention of the rest of the country. In 1909, the city put on the $10 million, 138-day Alaska-Yukon-Pacific Exposition, a cultural and trade fair, which was held on the grounds of the University of Washington. The event attracted 3.7 million patrons, including President William Howard Taft and the legendary orator William Jennings Bryan. Between 1900 and 1910, the city's population tripled from 80,761 to 237,194—while the state's population more than doubled—from 518,000 to 1,142,000 (including 32,000 Swedes). In 1914, with war beginning in Europe, Seattle became a shipbuilding center in the country. That same year saw the completion of the tallest edifice west of Chicago, the forty-two-story Smith Tower, named after the typewriter baron, L.C. Smith of Smith-Corona. By 1918, Seattle was connected by rail to the rest of the country by the Great Northern, the Northern Pacific, the Union Pacific, and the Chicago & Milwaukee railroads.

■ A Family Business

John and Hilda had five children: Everett W., Elmer J., Lloyd N., Mabel, and Esther. In 1915, twelve-year-old Everett and eleven-year-old Elmer began helping out in the store on Second and Pike. Elmer's first job was as a "button boy." He recounted that experience in *A Winning Team,* a privately published family history:

> In those days women wore high button shoes and to achieve a good fit, the buttons usually had to be adjusted for each customer. The clerk would mark the new positions for the buttons with a pencil, then hand them to one of the

button boys. On busy days, there were as many as three of us in the back adjusting buttons while the customers waited for their shoes. We cut the buttons off by hand, then used a machine with a foot stamp to reposition them.

In 1923, Wallin & Nordstrom opened their second store, in northeast Seattle, near the University of Washington campus. Everett, who had just graduated from the university at age twenty, was in charge of the opening. He managed the store for some years, until he left to become the West Coast sales representative for the J.P. Smith Shoe Company of Chicago, a wholesale men's and women's shoe manufacturer. He was succeeded as store manager by Elmer, who had spent almost a year learning how to merchandise and sell shoes at Marshall Field & Company, the giant Chicago store, whose eight separate shoe departments easily dwarfed tiny Wallin & Nordstrom. "I came from a small store, where every shoe was a jewel," recalled Elmer, who was horrified at how shabbily Field employees handled the merchandise. He saw them remove the shoes from the stockroom and "just slide them down" to the sales floor. One time, Elmer and a dozen co-workers were assigned to match up three or four hundred cases of mismated shoes. Elmer was appalled at the loss of revenue represented by those mismatched shoes—as well as Marshall Field's cavalier attitude about that loss. When Elmer returned to Seattle, his father asked him what he had learned from his time at the great department store. "In all honesty," he said, "I did not bring back a lot of good ideas about what I should be doing in the retail business. But I certainly learned several things I should *not* do." His father replied, "In that case, you learned quite a bit."

Bruce Nordstrom, Everett's son, smiles at his uncle's story. "We probably have more mismated shoes today just

because we do that much more business. But you can't
get so calloused to it that you accept it. That's what discouraged Elmer." As a young boy, Bruce had an experience similar to Elmer's. "When I was a kid, I took a trip
to New York and went to Macy's shoe department. It was
the biggest shoe department I had ever seen in my life,"
Bruce recalled. Visiting Macy's at the end of the day, he
was amazed at what he saw: Workers wielding large mo-
torized sweepers clearing away dozens of pairs of old
shoes that people had left after they had purchased (or
stolen) new ones. The abandoned shoes were then packed
into large boxes and thrown away. "That's just accepting
the inevitable" costs of *shrinkage*—the retailing term for
losses due to pilferage, record-keeping errors, and incorrectly recorded sales. "You just can't do that" because
shrinkage seriously affects profits. Nordstom's shrinkage is under 1.5 percent of sales, about half the national
department store average. Bruce Nordstrom credited that
low figure to the diligence of Nordstrom employees, who
derive some of their compensation from profit sharing.
"It goes back to a feeling of ownership in the company.
Our people are saying, 'That's my merchandise. Don't
you steal from me!'"

The partnership between John Nordstrom and Carl
Wallin eventually soured, and by 1928, John convinced
twenty-five-year-old Everett and twenty-four-year-old
Elmer to buy out his interest in the company (consisting
of a couple of stores, employing about a dozen clerks) for
about $60,000 each. A year later, Wallin sold his share to
Everett and Elmer. The brothers owned the business only
on paper because their father had loaned them the money
for the purchase and had co-signed a bank note to ensure them working capital. In 1930, they renovated the
Second Avenue store by tripling the display and merchandising area, replacing the linoleum on the sales floor

with carpeting, improving lighting with new chande-
liers and fixtures, and installing comfortable upholstered chairs in coverings that blended with the soft
tones of the silver-gray oak cabinet work. In the middle
of the store, a sign that was prominently hung from the
ceiling read, "If We Sell You Well, Tell Others. If Not, Tell
Us." A basement area was created to sell lower-priced
shoes. The grand opening, August 19, 1930, marked the
change of the name of the store to Nordstrom's. Long
lines of customers waited to have their feet worked on by
a representative of a nationally known Canadian foot
specialist, Dr. Locke, who maintained that he could cor-
rect problem feet with a few basic adjustments. Locke
also designed men's and women's corrective shoes that
would supposedly straighten out crooked toes. "Many
claimed that he helped them a great deal . . . and we did
well with the shoes. They certainly helped our business," Elmer recalled. (Dr. Locke shoes are still manu-
factured today.)

The Great Depression didn't adversely affect Seattle
and its lumber-dependent economy until 1931, when
construction in the United States came to a virtual halt.
Shantytowns called "Hoovervilles" (named after then-
President Herbert C. Hoover) dotted the city, which was
itself bankrupt from the costs of local relief plans. Consumer buying power was stifled. People chose to resole
their shoes rather than buy new ones, causing the price
of shoes (and everything else) to plummet, and forcing
retailers to slash their profit margins. "Everett and I felt
that if the time ever came that my father's interests were
jeopardized, we would close, liquidate the business, so
that he would get his cash out and wouldn't lose anything," Elmer recalled. Business finally got so bad that
they decided to give themselves one more month before
calling it quits. "The next month picked up a little bit

and we were off to the races. But if it hadn't picked up, we would have closed up that month and there wouldn't have been a Nordstrom."

In 1933, the Pacific Northwest economy began to slowly climb out of its morass, helped by President Franklin Roosevelt's New Deal programs, which brought in much needed federal money for construction of projects such as public hospitals, housing projects, and the Grand Coulee Dam on the Columbia River.

■ Everett, Elmer, and Lloyd

The Nordstrom brothers were entrepreneurs; under-funded ones at that, so they did the most uncomplicated and the most obvious thing to get ahead—they worked hard. As the owners, "we felt that we should work harder than anyone else," said Elmer. "If we didn't, our lack-adaisical attitude would spread to the next level, and the next level on down until everyone was taking it easy." Unable to afford a janitor, the brothers arrived early every morning to vacuum the carpets and wash the outside of the windows. "Once in a while we would trim the windows, then try to rearrange the shoes in an interesting fashion." Over the years, as their sons and then their grandsons went to work at Nordstrom, they all performed similar housekeeping chores before they were ever allowed to actually sell shoes on the sales floor. To this day, even if your name is Nordstrom, you start your career at the bottom, along with everyone else.

After graduating from the University of Washington (as had his brothers) in 1932, Lloyd Nordstrom decided to join the business. Although Elmer and Everett questioned whether the store could generate sufficient income to support all three and their families, they nevertheless welcomed their baby brother and asked their accountant to figure the net worth of the business; whatever it was, Lloyd would purchase a one-third interest. A week later, the accountant came back with the grim news: Everett and Elmer, who had leveraged themselves to buy the store from their father in the middle of the Great Depression, had virtually no net worth. They had worked "night and day" for nearly four years and "hadn't made a nickel," recalled Elmer. "But at least we had the business."

The three Nordstrom brothers—whom employees referred to as "Mr. Everett," "Mr. Elmer," and "Mr. Lloyd"—created an effective combination, with each man's temperament and abilities, ideas, and working habits complemented by the others. "I can't think of one of the three brothers without thinking of the other two," said Bruce Nordstrom. "They weren't the same people, mind you. They certainly had three separate personalities."

Everett, the eldest, was the level-headed leader. "Everyone respected him," said Jack McMillan, one of the current co-chairmen. "He was a very forceful, strong person in his beliefs, his attitudes, and his old-fashioned virtues." In the 1930s, when an earthquake jolted the store and overturned displays, "everyone started to panic," Elmer recalled. But then they were calmed at the sight of Everett "standing by the elevator with his arms folded, a calming smile on his face." A high school graduate at sixteen and a college graduate at twenty, Everett was the financial specialist (as well as a sports statistics enthusiast). "Everett really watched the pennies carefully," recalled co-chairman John N. Nordstrom, Everett's nephew. "When I came into the business, one of the first things he told me was that [for the business] we should watch every single penny and keep things as efficient as possible. But when you get home [to your family and private life], that's where you spend it. That advice stuck with me."

Everett also had a reputation for being a stickler for merchandise quality. Once, when the uppers (the parts of the shoe above the toe) of a group of women's pumps were separating from the soles, Everett notified the manufacturer, who told Everett to send back the defective ones. To ensure that no customer would have a problem with the pumps, Everett popped the soles of *every* shoe from that delivery, and then shipped them all back to the manufacturer. Ever since, Nordstrom has had a reputation for being a thorn in the side of most manufacturers because Nordstrom buyers are supposed to go over every piece of merchandise with the proverbial fine-toothed comb. If it isn't perfect, Nordstrom won't sell it. "Nordstrom is great for the customer, but murder for the manufacturer. I hate selling them," an anonymous manufacturer told *Footwear News*, "but I'd hate it even more if we didn't sell them."

Some shoe vendors once complained in an article on Nordstrom in *Footwear News* that Nordstrom forced them to take shoes back "unconditionally." In an interview for this book, Bruce Nordstrom challenged that assertion and said that returns should be judged on a case-by-case basis. Because Nordstrom realizes that some customers will take advantage of its unconditional return policy, the company instructs its merchandisers to be careful not to send back each and every pair of returned shoes. "Don't pass that mistake on to the vendor," said Bruce Nordstrom. "On the other hand, [vendors] know that we are liberal with our customers. And if you're going to do business with us, then there should be a liberal influence on their return policies. If somebody has worn a shoe, and it doesn't wear satisfactorily for them, and we think that person is being honest about it, then we will send it back. It's not a science; it's a feel." He said he cautions his merchandisers not to use Nordstrom's economic might "as a stick and beat these poor people. We're the big guys now, but I remember when we were the little guys and how high-handed the big guys were with us. We shouldn't be high-handed." Nevertheless, one can still hear those complaints from vendors, who don't think that Bruce's message has been heard by some Nordstrom buyers.

Elmer, the tall, lanky, middle brother, was the mechanically inclined, detail man. He supervised store planning and operations, monitored inventories, negotiated with the sales clerk union from the 1930s until he retired in 1968, and bought men's, boys, and children's shoes. "Elmer was a lower-keyed guy with a good sense of humor, and was beloved in family circles," said Jack McMillan. In his later years, as the last surviving brother, he represented Nordstrom's institutional memory. At directors' meetings, shareholders' meetings, and store openings, Elmer, an engaging raconteur, was often called upon to tell stories of the old days, particularly to make a point about the company and the family. One story he enjoyed telling had to do with respect for his father. When he was sixteen, Elmer traveled 225 miles to Spokane, Washington, to drive back a rare, 1920 Premier automobile that his father had ordered. Coming back to Seattle, Elmer was accompanied by a Nordstrom salesman, who was expecting a fast trip home in the new vehicle. But he hadn't counted on Elmer's following his father's precise instructions to not drive the car over twenty miles an hour. "I had to remind that poor fellow that I had strict orders," Elmer recalled. The trip took more than eighteen hours.

The personable Lloyd was the most outgoing of the brothers and represented the company's public persona as the director of advertising and publicity operations.

Lloyd shared with Everett the buying and merchandising of women's shoes (the bulk of the business) and also took his turn managing the University District store. Lloyd was the best athlete of the brothers. As an undergraduate at the University of Washington (were he was class president), he was a nationally ranked intercollegiate tennis player and played center on the varsity basketball team. He competed in singles and doubles at the national tennis championships at Forest Hills, New York, and was invited to play on the United States Davis Cup Team. When the great Don Budge competed in Seattle, he played against Lloyd Nordstrom. Lloyd was a mentor for many men and women throughout the Nordstrom organization, and was later one of the prime movers in bringing professional football to Seattle, with the expansion team, the Seahawks. "Lloyd was an imposing figure," John N. Nordstrom described his uncle. "He liked the designers and the social events, and being quoted in the newspaper. There was even some talk about his running for governor." Jack McMillan described his father-in-law as an "old school kind of a gentleman. He had a veneer of calm, gentle spirit, but he was very competitive."

Like all successful entrepreneurs, the three brothers shared a single-minded devotion to the business. On busy days, while two brothers sold shoes, the other monitored the activity on the sales floor. They did not join the Seattle service clubs and organizations because they didn't have the time to attend the lunch-hour meetings. They never went to lunch together because their policy was that one of them should be present in the store at all times—even on autumn Saturdays when their beloved University of Washington Huskies were playing football. At the end of the day, they were the last ones to leave the store.

Ironically, the brothers weren't particularly good at moving the merchandise out of the store. "Dad's probably the worst salesman in the business," Lloyd once admitted to a Seattle newspaper, "and the only ones that could be worse are his three sons." Nevertheless, he added, "If we can give better selection and better value, we can afford to be poor salesmen." This philosophy continues today. With the exception of James F. Nordstrom, none of the current Nordstrom family members was particularly strong on the sales floor; instead, they hire people who are and act as cheerleaders to encourage those people. The brothers were constantly walking through the stores, talking to the employees on the floor, thanking them for doing a good job, and reiterating that they were valued, that their hard work was appreciated. "Whatever we needed, we got," recalled Pat Kennedy, corporate merchandise manager of men's shoes, who began working for the company in the late 1960s. "There was always a very high expectation level and we felt there was no limit to what we could do. They empowered us to make our own decisions, and supported us in those decisions. If something was wrong, we had the authority to immediately fix it. Even if we failed, we weren't criticized. So, with that support, many of us had a strong desire to go the extra mile."

The Nordstrom brothers continually emphasized that most basic retailing rule—*the customer is always right*—and underscored the importance of sales associates giving extra attention to every customer, even the difficult ones. Elmer often told the story of one salesman who came to work in a grumpy mood because he had had a hard time with a customer the day before. "You can wait on twenty customers and they are all friendly except one," Elmer told the salesman. "So you might go home at night remembering only the bad one and forget about the nineteen who were so good. It should be the other way around."

■ Decision by Consensus

Perhaps the Nordstrom brothers' biggest strength was that, by all reports, they genuinely liked each other and got along well and, just as important, so did their wives. The brothers worked side by side in an office so tiny that their desks were squeezed together like a size 11 foot in a size 10 shoe. They would meet at least once a week with their families to discuss the shoe business, which was virtually their whole life. They enjoyed the friendly fraternal competition and each wanted to be successful in his own area of the business. "We wanted to be the best that we could. We had no prizes, and we didn't boast about it, but we always knew which brother was doing the best. Knowing that only made the other two try harder," said Elmer. They all lived very carefully, drawing out just enough money to live on. "At the end of the year, we could see how much money we spent," recalled Elmer. "If I spent more [in his area of responsibility] than my other brothers, I'd have to drop a little bit [the next year] because we all wanted to be the same."

Official corporate titles didn't become a legal requirement until the company was incorporated in 1938, which was a year after they moved uptown into a new, larger store on Fifth Avenue between Pike and Pine streets. Everett, as the eldest, was the natural choice for president, but before he would take the post, he had one condition: the posts of president, vice-president, and secretary/treasurer should be rotated every two years. "People would ask us our titles and we sometimes had trouble remembering who was who on that day," said Elmer. "The only time it meant anything was when we had to sign some papers. We had to look up and see who was president." Today, because Nordstrom is a public company, titles are official.

Decision-by-consensus management originated in the difficult days of the 1930s. Early on, the brothers realized that their ability to work well together was crucial to the success of the business. Their relationship was akin to a marriage. "You worked together for a common goal, but you didn't get your own way all the time," said Elmer. Options were weighed and discussed as a team. Disagreements were resolved by majority rule. Bruce Nordstrom observed that the brothers formulated strategies and reached conclusions because they were "on the same wavelength . . . and on the same page." Today, that same philosophy is shared by the current generation of Nordstroms. (Their approach will be discussed in detail in Chapter 3.)

■ Growth by Necessity

With the advent of World War II, Everett, Elmer, and Lloyd found merchandise was scarce because much of the leather supply and domestic footwear production were earmarked for military use. Retailers were assigned a quota of shoes they could sell, and many stores closed up shop (even in the middle of the day) once they met their daily quota. Store buyers routinely doubled their usual orders in order to ensure delivery of half of what they needed. The Nordstrom brothers were able to sell virtually every pair of shoes they could get their hands on, including women's work shoes, which became a new merchandise staple. And they could sell those shoes without having to mark them down from the original retail price. That meant they made money on every pair they sold. (One Christmas, a desperate customer bought two right-footed men's slippers when the store had sold out of a popular style.) Armed with their checkbooks, the brothers crisscrossed the country by train, calling on factories to beg and cajole for extra shoes. Whenever traveling shoe salesmen arrived in Seattle, the brothers usually bought them lunch and often brought them home for dinner. "The salesmen usually had good personalities due to the nature of their jobs . . . and because they traveled so much, they usually had plenty of entertaining stories," Elmer recalled. Not surprisingly, when a salesman found himself with extra pairs to sell, he often offered them first to the Nordstroms. By the time the war was over in 1945, Nordstrom had became a nationally recognized shoe power, famous for aggressive buys and huge inventories.

To secure a regular supply of odd sizes, the Nordstrom brothers had to convince manufacturers to invest in expensive, special equipment to make larger shoes. (Shoes are made over a "last." Each length and width in almost every style requires a special last.) As Nordstrom's volume increased, "the factories were happy to make the investment, especially because they could charge us more for larger sizes," recalled Elmer. "Though these shoes cost us more, we always offered them at the same price or a fraction more than the regular sizes." It was good advertising. Nordstrom buyers worked closely with manufacturers to obtain the best values, unique items, and the widest selections. That same approach continues today.

Expansion was the only way the brothers could support their three growing families and attract motivated employees with opportunities for advancement. In the early 1950s, Nordstrom took over leased department-store shoe operations in Tacoma, Portland, Oakland, Fresno, Sacramento, Albuquerque, Phoenix, San Antonio, and Honolulu, where they bought the merchandise, hired the salespeople, and paid a percentage of every sale to the stores that leased Nordstrom the space. (They learned that most department stores were poor merchandisers of footwear, which requires a greater outlay of capital and deeper inventories than apparel.)

At the same time, they continued to open their own stores in Washington state and Oregon, and remodeled and expanded the four-floor downtown flagship store. In the early 1960s, the Seattle store became the largest independently owned shoe store in the United States, with annual sales of $12 million. The store stocked 150,000 pairs, with the widest selection of sizes and widths in the world, from 2½ to 14, AAAAAA to E, for women; 5 to 18, AAA to EEE, for men, in a broad range of colors. If an item was hot, Nordstrom had more of it than anybody. Nordstrom, in the words of Bruce Nordstrom, "had to be literally all things to all people. We had to have little old ladies' shoes and hookers' shoes and cheap shoes and expensive shoes. That was counter to all the advice you would get from the industry. The industry was always telling you to target your customers and go after them. But our goal was to sell shoes to everyone in Seattle." (In fact, one out of every four Seattle women bought their shoes at Nordstrom.) John N. Nordstrom told *Footwear News*. "Better not miss a size, better be nice and have the right styles. We have tried to copy that system. We don't try to have only the biggest selection or the best prices. We have got to do everything."

Elmer Nordstrom, John N.'s father, recalled, "We worked on closer margins and never took as large a markup as our competitors. For that reason, other stores did not want to carry the same shoes as we did because they knew we would probably undersell them. If a customer came to us and said, 'I can buy this for a better price at another store,' we would meet the lower price." Today, Nordstrom continues that philosophy. Shoppers entering a Nordstrom store today will see signs that proclaims,

"Nordstrom will not be undersold," and will match the price of any comparable item sold at the competition.

Nordstrom also repaired shoes. One notable customer in need was a tourist from Memphis, Tennessee, Elvis Presley, who was in Seattle in 1962 to film "Meet Me At the World's Fair." One afternoon, Colonel Tom Parker, Elvis's manager, came running into the store carrying a pair of pointed boots that had split open on the sides. The colonel told Elmer Nordstrom that Elvis was across the street in his stocking feet, surrounded by excited female fans. "We took them down to our shoe repair department and gave them V.I.P. treatment," Elmer recalled. "You couldn't have the King of Rock'n Roll walking around outside Nordstrom's without a pair of shoes."

KEYS TO SUCCESS

The principles by which Nordstrom is run today were instituted from the 1920s through the 1950s by Everett, Elmer, and Lloyd Nordstrom, the sons of the founder, John W. Nordstrom. Nordstrom began as a small, independent retailer and has continued to run the business with that same level of personal care. This attitude is reflected in the following ways:

- Stocking high-quality merchandise and treating every item "like a jewel."
- Buyers work closely with manufacturers in order to obtain the best values, unique items, and the widest selections of styles and prices, from the economical to the extravagant.
- Nordstrom can be a thorn in the side of manufacturers. Buyers go over every piece of merchandise with a "fine-toothed comb."
- Salespeople must have a complete understanding of the product and its selling points.
- "The customer is always right" is not a cliche at Nordstrom.
- Decision-by-consensus is how the Nordstrom brothers ran their business. Working together in a relationship akin to a marriage, they freely ventilated their opinions. Disagreements were worked out behind closed doors and a united front was presented to the public. That philosophy is shared by the current generation of Nordstrom family co-chairmen.

The Next Generation

Perfecting "The Nordstrom Way"

By the early 1960s, the third generation of Nordstroms had become key management players. This group of vice-presidents, who at the time were all in their thirties, was comprised of Everett's son, Bruce A., Elmer's two sons, James F. and John N., and John A. "Jack" McMillan, who was married to Lloyd's daughter, Loyal, and represented Lloyd's one-third interest in the company. All four were University of Washington graduates, with degrees in business. Like their fathers, the three younger Nordstroms began working in the store as children, and continued to sell shoes throughout high school and college; McMillan was first employed as an undergraduate. All of them toiled for years in the stockroom before, Bruce said, their fathers "ever allowed us near a foot."

Trained from the sales floor, the third generation was literally and figuratively "raised kneeling in front of the customer," said Bruce, who uses that phrase "because it says more than one thing. First, it obviously speaks to worshiping the customer and appreciating that that's where our living comes from. We wouldn't be here without

63

the customer. The other thing is that the shoe business is the dirtiest, hardest, most physically difficult part of the soft-goods business because you have to handle the inventory so much. In every other form of soft-goods retailing, most of the inventory is out on the floor, but in the case of footwear, you have to go get it in the backroom. You have to decipher what the customer has in her head. And then you have the size element: the foot is the most difficult part of the anatomy to fit. You've got to have the right size; you've got to have what they want and when they want it. So, there you are trying to do these things—humble, sweating, on your knees."

■ Diversifying into Apparel

To create opportunities for the younger Nordstroms to stay with the company, the brothers felt they had to either open more shoe stores outside the Pacific Northwest (which they had outgrown) or diversify into another business. Lloyd Nordstrom wanted to move into women's apparel. He argued that it required less capital investment in inventory than shoes, generated better turnover and profit, and would perfectly complement their shoe business. On a personal level, Elmer recalled, "Lloyd had the feeling, because he came in late, that he didn't have as strong a part in building the business as the two of us, which was a mistake, of course." Jack McMillan noted, "Going into apparel was something that I don't think any of us could have conceived of if Lloyd hadn't had this need to do his own thing. He was living a comfortable life at that time, but he had this competitive drive that got him involved in a new business at an age [fifty-three] where he didn't really need to do that."

The Nordstroms aimed their sights on Best's Apparel, Inc., a fashionable downtown Seattle retailer (with a second store in downtown Portland), whose motto was

"Specialists in smart apparel for young women of all ages." After pursuing Best's for several years, Lloyd Nordstrom consummated the transaction in August 1963. At the time, the two Best's stores were annually generating a combined $7 million worth of sales volume, but were losing $2 million.

The Nordstroms almost didn't get the Best's stores. Ivan Best initially offered the stores to William S. Street, who in 1962 retired as president of Frederick & Nelson. Street declined, but then asked executives at Marshall Field & Company, the parent company of Frederick & Nelson, if they were interested in Best's; they were not. If Street or Marshall Field had acquired Best, the Nordstrom story would have taken a very different turn. As it was, the deal, which had to be approved by all three of the brothers, almost became a casualty of the Nordstroms' decision-by-consensus approach. The final discussions were held in Everett's office, where the two generations of Nordstroms convened. The only one missing was Elmer, who was out of town but was in contact by telephone. When the brothers asked Elmer what he thought of the terms of the deal, the middle brother dissented. "We really don't know the apparel business," he said. "I think we ought to do what we know how to do and expand, maybe into San Francisco, with shoe stores." Lloyd, who had spent four years negotiating with Ivan Best, simply said, "Fine. We won't do it." That response took Elmer by surprise. "Wait a minute," Elmer replied. "If you guys want to do it, then we'll do it." Jim Nordstrom, who attended that meeting, recalled that it made a big impression on him: "They got into a heckuva an argument, deferring to each other, trying to honor the other guy's wishes. I thought that was a good lesson to all of us."

Two months after the Best deal was made founder John W. Nordstrom died of a cerebral hemorrhage at the age of ninety-two. Although he officially retired in 1928, when he was fifty-seven, he maintained an office in the store, coming in almost every day, to play cards or cribbage with friends or just to walk around the store. A customer who mistook him for a clerk once commented, "I know these Nordstrom boys are loyal to their employees, but I can't understand why they keep working that old man." Whenever friends asked John W. if he hadn't taken a big risk by putting virtually all his net worth into the hands of his relatively inexperienced sons, he replied, "I only went through the sixth grade in grammar school in Sweden. My boys are college graduates. They must be a lot smarter than I ever was."

Today, every year, the top Nordstrom manager is given the John W. Nordstrom Award for possessing the same traits John W. demonstrated during his lifetime.

■ ■ ■

The brothers believed that if you could run a shoe store, you could run any business. But their entry into apparel was initially greeted with skepticism by manufacturers who "weren't very enthused to see us on buying trips," recalled Elmer, "but that only reminded us of our early days in shoes. It was like starting over in many ways, and that was exciting. No one really believed that shoe store owners could be successful with apparel. No one, except us." The apparel industry's reservations about Nordstrom continued for almost a decade. Cynthia C. Paur, who today is Nordstrom's corporate merchandise manager for better ready-to-wear women's apparel, recalled that when she first became a buyer (when Nordstrom had only five stores), "we had a difficult time securing a lot of the hot lines that we wanted to buy. We were the little guy." And when Nordstrom did manage to secure those lines, which everyone else was carrying, "the only way we could attract attention was to [price] them for a dollar less." Those first few years in the apparel business were such an expensive learning experience for the Nordstroms that "Everett and Elmer were asking Lloyd what he had gotten us into," recalled Jack McMillan, who helped his father-in-law get Best's going. There were a lot of markdowns (reductions from the original retail prices), and the business wasn't as profitable as they thought it was going to be. They wanted to know when Lloyd was going to get this thing figured out. But Lloyd had a vision, and was determined that we were going to be successful."

To oversee the buying of women's apparel, Nordstrom hired a man who was well regarded in the industry. "We marveled at him. He was just what we thought a dress buyer ought to be," Bruce Nordstrom told *Forbes* magazine in 1978. "But one day we were having a meeting to plan our normal [internal] sales contest and we said, 'All right, the winners get steak and the losers get beans.' Well, I was walking out behind this guy and he turned to someone and said, 'This is the most sophomoric thing I've ever heard.' I guess it was, but he was at the bottom of all our performance lists." Although he was "a substantial guy in the industry, he was not for us." From then on, Nordstrom has had a policy of never hiring managers from the outside because Nordstrom believes that a person can appreciate the culture only by growing up in it. The regional manager, the store manager, the department manager, and so on, know what the salespeople need because they were once salespeople. By the same token, Nordstrom, with the exception of the 1975 acquisition of three stores in Alaska, does not acquire other retailers because it is too difficult, costly, and time-consuming to change the existing culture.

Nordstrom did pick up one valuable idea from Best's: a preseason Anniversary Sale featuring new (rather than end-of-season) merchandise. "Best's had started it in order to provide business for the slowest time of the year, which was in the month of July," recalled Bruce Nordstrom. "Basically, what they did was bring in some special-purchase fall items. We thought it was a good idea, but we thought it would be an even better idea to bring in the best stuff. We did that, and it really made the difference." Today, Nordstrom places that merchandise (along with special purchases) on sale for a ten-day period; after that, it is marked back up to regular price. Many retailers across the country have copied this idea, "But they all miss homing in on just the best items," said Bruce Nordstrom. "That's what we do."

■ Expansion: Creating a Fast Career Track

With the next generation getting more involved in day-to-day affairs, Everett, Elmer, and Lloyd were free to look at the big picture: expansion sites, financing, and leases. The brothers saw an opportunity to outmaneuver Frederick & Nelson, whose parent company, Marshall Field & Company, was timid in expanding F&N to the suburbs, leaving Nordstrom Best (the new name of the company) to fill the better-apparel niche in the Seattle area. In 1965, Nordstrom Best built its first combination apparel and shoe store in Seattle's Northgate Shopping Center, one of the first shopping malls in the United States. The following year, the company purchased a Portland fashion shop called Nicholas Ungar, which it merged with its downtown Portland shoe store. Stores soon followed in Tacoma and suburban Seattle.

Led by the younger generation, Nordstrom had rejuvenated itself into a young-thinking company, even though it had already been in business for more than six decades. Expansion created a fast career track for energetic, entrepreneurial young people, who were rewarded for their performance with increased responsibility and advancement. Promoting from within became an essential ingredient in Nordstrom's success. Homegrown associates appreciated, understood, maintained, and spread the culture to new stores and regions. "We did everything we could to get the best people, and once we had them, we did everything we could to keep them," recalled Elmer Nordstrom. "We wanted our people to know that they could work their way up, while also learning about the business on different levels." Some associates became buyers in their early twenties; one store manager was just twenty-three; one shoe buyer was a mere twenty.

Many of these buyers and managers were (and are) women. Because the Nordstroms knew that they did not know a lot about the women's apparel business, "they were very anxious to identify people who demonstrated a flair for women's apparel, and move them along," recalled Cynthia Paur, who began her career in 1968 doing stock work while still a college student. "There were many jobs available for women. It all depended on what career path you wanted to take, whether it was on the merchant side or the store management side. I have always felt that any job I wanted was open to me." Nordstrom has continued to be very aggressive in promoting women to high executive positions. Today, almost 40 percent of company officers and 66 percent of store managers are female. In 1994, Nordstrom was singled out for its positive policies toward women in the workplace in a study sponsored by Progressive Securities Financial Services of Seattle; the Women's Equity Mutual Fund of San Francisco; and Kinder, Lydenberg, Domini & Co. Inc., Cambridge, Massachusetts. The study considered several factors, including superior performance in advancement of women in positions and pay, progressive family-benefit programs, and use of women-owned suppliers.

Why are none of the Nordstrom women involved in the day-to-day operations of the company? The answer appears to center around their generation rather than their gender. The third generation of Nordstrom women, who grew up in the 1940s and 1950s, chose to be wives and homemakers, although during her college and post-graduate years, Anne E. Nordstrom Gittinger, Bruce's sister, worked for Nordstrom in the financial area. "She was by far the smarter of the two of us; more personable and more attractive," said Bruce. "Had she been born in this era, she would have been chairman of the board of this company." Today, Anne Gittinger chairs Nordstrom's corporate contribution committee.

■ ■ ■

Lloyd Nordstrom, the prime instigator for the move into women's wear, worked with the third generation to update the apparel store's image and merchandise in order to appeal to a younger group of fashion-conscious consumers, the Baby Boom generation. The plan was to reach them at the impressionable time when buying habits were being set. Men's wear, featuring suits and sportswear, was added in 1968 at the Bellevue Square store. "The Nordstrom name, with its long association with both men's and women's shoes, cast no fears of feminine frills and fragrances into stout-hearted men," wrote a footwear trade magazine. The move into men's wear was a natural for Nordstrom because it already had many salespeople in their footwear department; its combined shoe and apparel stores had a better balance of men and women sales people than most apparel specialty stores. Lloyd Nordstrom made no secret of his intentions. He told the *Seattle Times* that the company was "hopeful and optimistic of becoming one of the major men's divisions in the nation."

From 1963 to 1969, Nordstrom increased its gross sales 500 percent to $60 million.

■ A Changing of the Guard

In 1968, Everett turned sixty-five, which was the company's informal retirement age. The brothers were keenly aware of the fact that most companies eventually fail because older executives tended to shun risks. They didn't want that to happen to Nordstrom. "Employees won't find much incentive for coming up with new ideas if they know they'll be viewed by an older, conservative boss. The result is sometimes an old taskmaster, surrounded by 'Yes-Men,' rather than people who want to take charge and produce," said Elmer, who was to follow Everett into retirement two years later. "My father retired at fifty-seven and gave us our chance. Now our turns were coming up, even though we were in good health and capable of continuing."

Virtually all of the brothers' net worth and their only source of income was the corporation. Throughout their working lives, they had simply drawn out enough money to live on (all received the same salary) and had never paid themselves dividends, choosing instead to refunnel that money for further expansion. With retirement imminent, they wanted their estates to have a market value that could be readily established for the purpose of estate taxes. Their alternatives were to either sell the chain to the next generation or to an established retailer. Because the younger Nordstroms lacked the capital, the first option was not viable; but the second option was not only viable, it was preferable because it would make the brothers wealthy. They notified the third generation that they intended to sell the company, and soon Associated Dry Goods, Dayton Hudson Corporation, and Broadway-Hale Stores (the company later known as Carter Hawley Hale and today as Broadway Stores) emerged as the prominent suitors. Jack McMillan recalled that as the offers began coming in, he and the young Nordstroms were forced to ask themselves whether they wanted to work for one of those three retail giants and, "the more we thought about it, we didn't."

Broadway-Hale made the most financially appealing offer: a million shares of Broadway-Hale stock at approximately twenty-four dollars a share. The third generation, who would become significant Broadway-Hale stockholders, would continue to run the Nordstrom operation as a division of Broadway-Hale. For Jim Nordstrom, the most "sobering" experience came when he and his contemporaries were having lunch with Edward Carter, chairman of Broadway-Hale, who told the young Nordstroms how much he liked their stores and praised their ability to do well through tough times in Seattle. When he asked each of them how they were able to accomplish that, they explained that they simply used a decentralized management system. "John talked about the men's shoes business; Bruce about ladies shoes; Jack and I talked about apparel," Jim Nordstrom recalled. "After we got all through [talking about the company's decentralized approach and decision-by-consensus style], Ed Carter said, 'You can't run a business like that.' I think we then all realized our job security was in jeopardy."

Before the senior Nordstroms entered into an agreement with Broadway-Hale, the younger Nordstroms told them that they could do a better job of running the company than any outside organization. "We asked them to entrust their fortune to us," said Bruce. The brothers had their doubts. "They looked at us and they weren't thrilled with what they saw," Jim recollected. "So, the idea of [ensuring their] security and selling it to another company appealed to them." The brothers believed the main reason they had achieved their success was their ability to work together as a cohesive unit. They didn't know if the boys, who had always gotten along (but had not had the opportunity to work as a group) could duplicate that solidarity. "And we didn't want to see them break up into feuding factions trying to," recalled Elmer.

The third generation presented Everett, Elmer, and Lloyd with a detailed business plan and arguments that they could successfully run the business. They proposed to pay for the transaction by issuing stock and taking the company public. That would be an extraordinary move for a firm that prided itself on its very low profile and who had financed expansion solely out of earnings. "These guys were very private," said Jack McMillan. "Going public was not to their liking" because they believed that the pressures of quarter-to-quarter performance promoted short-term thinking. Prior to 1966, the company had never given Dun & Bradstreet a balance sheet or operating statement. "They were also afraid they were going to sell their stock to their friends and [the stock] would go down. That bothered them the most," said John N. Nordstrom. Despite their misgivings, the brothers, who were encouraged by the four boys' ability to organize themselves, accepted their proposal. "We were shocked," said Jim Nordstrom. "We thought they would take the money."

The pro forma proposal put together by the third generation estimated that Nordstrom would reach $100 million in sales by 1980. They underestimated that target figure by almost $400 million.

At a meeting in Seattle, the brothers informed Edward Carter, chairman of Broadway-Hale, of their decision.

After the meeting, Carter, a large, white-haired man who cut an impressive figure, came into Bruce's office and told him that he and his compatriots were "making a big mistake." He said that he didn't care how big Nordstrom ever got because Nordstrom's stock would never be as highly valued as Broadway-Hale stock, which, he said, "will always carry a premium." Bruce recalled, "I don't know if I believed it, but I thought to myself, 'Well, [maybe] you're going to be valued more than us, but I think we're better merchants than you are.' I didn't tell him that, but that was the basis of our confidence." Carter reminded Bruce that if the deal went through, the Nordstroms would be the biggest shareholders in Broadway-Hale and would be integral in running their stores. To Bruce, "That was not a selling point. Although his stores were successful, we weren't thrilled with them and didn't want to run them."

Unable to acquire Nordstrom, Broadway-Hale later acquired the Bergdorf Goodman chain. Today, the total market value of Nordstrom is more than thirty times greater than what it would have been if it had been acquired by Broadway-Hale. Broadway Stores eventually filed for bankruptcy in 1990; the value of its stock, at this writing, is worth one-seventh of Nordstrom stock.

■ ■ ■

In May 1970, operating management was assumed by Bruce, then thirty-seven; John, thirty-four; Jim, thirty-one; and Jack McMillan, thirty-nine. The following year, the three Nordstroms became co-presidents and directors, and drew the same salary. Bruce merchandised women's shoes and (like his father, Everett) dealt with bankers and investors; John handled men's wear and store planning; Jim was responsible for sportswear, juniors, and children's wear; and executive vice-president McMillan handled women's ready-to-wear. Robert Bender, a longtime acquaintance of the Nordstroms (and another University of Washington graduate), who was an up-and-coming young executive with J.C. Penney, was put in charge of accessories. Elmer, Everett, and Lloyd became co-chairmen of the board, "offering encouragement and resisting the temptation to give advice," wrote Elmer. As the torch was passed, the older brothers emphasized the need for constant diligence, "because from our experience during the war years, we saw how easily a business could fall apart from neglect." They gave the boys a long list of potential excuses that included the weather, the economy, and the new shopping center down the block. "We told them they might as well give us their excuses by the number, because they didn't mean a thing. If business was bad, there was nowhere to put the blame but upon themselves."

Like their predecessors, the third generation represented a variety of personalities who shared a common goal and a genuine love of the business.

Some say John can be the toughest of the three Nordstroms in terms of setting the standards for how things should be done. He "likes to have a good time, and he leaves people alone, but when he tells you something, that's it—it's law. And if it's not done, he can be very unforgiving," a source told *Women's Wear Daily.* Bob Bender said that in discussions on decisions, John "sometimes plays the 'black hat'; the one who would be hardest to convince."

Bruce described his cousin John as "probably the most focused and most targeted of the four of us. So whenever he gets a bee in his bonnet about something, you know that it will be researched and thought about from every angle. Because of his nature, he will question whatever we're all excited about. So we then have to respond to his questions." Jim Nordstrom agreed. Because his brother John is "analytical," he "kept us out of a lot of bad deals because he spots things that we, in our enthusiasm, wouldn't spot. He enjoys playing the adversarial role. He also enjoys the nitty gritty, the store planning, figuring the cost of every light bulb."

Bruce, observers say, brings a love of the shoe business, which continues to be a key element of the Nordstrom operation, accounting for 20 percent of total sales. In a cover story for *Footwear News,* which elected him the industry's 1987 man of the year, Bruce was described as "either a very complex man or a very simple man . . . a caring man rooted in bedrock family values, as well as a modest, private person"—so much so that he declined to be interviewed for the story because it would draw attention to him personally. "Bruce, like his father [Everett] . . . operates on merit," Philip Barach, chairman of U.S. Shoe Corporation told *Footwear News.* "He likes doing business with people who can deliver." Bob Bender said that, "If something bad is said about the company, while they all hurt, I think Bruce shows it the most."

Jim is considered the most fun-loving and easy going of the group, as well as the best salesman and the most entertaining raconteur. "Jim's probably brought a little more zip and joie de vivre. He has an instinctive feeling about retailing," said Bruce. "Jim has been very effective in the fashion end of the business. He's also a real good pilot. I've had chief pilots call Jim a natural; he just has a feel." As the youngest of the three Nordstroms, Jim identified most closely with Lloyd, who was the youngest of the three brothers. Annette Armony, a Nordstrom sales associate, recalled the time when Jim came into her department at the Portland store and a rounder (a circular merchandise rack) fell down. "Denim was all over the floor. He helped us pick up the merchandise. He was so cool about it. He said, 'something's wrong with this rounder, let's go in the back room and get a new one.'"

When it comes to making group decisions, Jim Nordstrom said that usually, "You see Bruce and me voting the same. Our personalities and personal lives are similar. We like the same things. You could put a hat over us."

Jack McMillan brings a non-Nordstrom-family point of view to the executive suite. A director since 1966, McMillan was elected president in May 1988—the first time a Nordstrom family member did not occupy that office. "Jack's one of the best human relations guys that I've ever seen," said Bruce. "He has a good feel for people and how to motivate them. He's great on goal setting."

Because they share common goals, this generation of Nordstroms has had no problem emulating their predecessors' decision-by-consensus approach. "Any major decision—for that matter, any minor decision—that we make in this company, if the family can't sign off on it, then we won't do it," said Bruce Nordstrom.

"We have our differences," McMillan admitted. "You swallow your ego for the long-term good of the company. We've all had to do that. We've all had our turn to be frustrated. Instead of breaking things up, you ultimately decide to get in line and do what's best for the group."

Bruce Nordstrom said that the company has "probably been prevented from making some errors because one of us said, 'That just doesn't sound right.' The others respect that one vote enough that [we will] go in another direction. You would think that maybe that would cause inaction. But it so happens, probably because of the example those three [brothers] set, it really causes action." He claimed that he and the other co-chairmen have had very few instances of serious disagreement on major business subjects. "It comes from the fact that we were all raised the same and went through the same experiences. Your backgrounds and thoughts tend to be the same. Of course, we're not the same people; we have different personalities. But the input is kind of the same. So, when decisions came, we all tended to arrive at the same conclusion," he said. "I can tell you a number of times that we had decisions on building stores, where we could get three yeas and one nay. Our system is that if it's a strong enough nay, we don't do it." In practice, the three yeas lobby the one nay.

One example, in the early 1990s, was the decision to build a store in the giant Mall of America in Bloomington, Minnesota. One of the co-chairmen felt that because the Minneapolis-based Dayton Hudson department store chain was "such an institution in Minneapolis, that it would be like butting our head against the wall. Their thing was what our thing is: involvement in our towns, being respectful of each individual and worshiping the customer. And they had this big head start," said Bruce Nordstrom. But unlike Nordstrom, the Dayton family was no longer involved in the operation of Dayton Hudson, which is run by professional managers. "Our company is run by the Nordstroms," Bruce continued, "we have our name over the door. The manager at the Mall of America is my son, Erik. People are parochial enough and Scandinavian enough in that town that they love going to that store. (In fact, there are many more Nordstroms listed in the Twin Cities phonebook than the Seattle phonebook.) They see Erik Nordstrom; they can talk to him. There's something to that. I think that's what caused us, as a committee, to win those [nay] votes over."

The Nordstroms readily agree that the company would not have been as successful if only one of them were in charge. "We've worked together our whole lives, and it's such second nature to us, and we unconsciously lean on each other's strengths without being able to talk about it," said Bruce. "There's no question that, as a committee, the four of us, by being a cohesive committee, bring a much stronger single presence to the office of the CEO, because we all have little things that we probably do some better than other people. We've seen time and again what works and what doesn't work. So, you're kind of focused in on the merchandising end. We're all merchants. Among the four of us, we have no financial expertise; we have no personnel expertise. But we all share merchandising expertise. Everett, Elmer, and Lloyd were the same way."

Can other companies emulate this decision-by-consensus approach?

Yes, if all parties involved park their egos outside the boardroom, trust each other, and share the common goal of doing what's best for the company—not necessarily what's best for themselves.

"There is a notable absence of politics at Nordstrom. Yes, there is some at different levels, but it is far more muted than in other companies," said Alfred E. Osborne, Jr., a member of the Nordstrom board of directors, who is director of the Entrepreneurial Studies Center and Associate Professor of Business Economics in The John E. Anderson Graduate School of Management of the University of California, Los Angeles. Osborne noted that the Nordstroms "put the time in up front to hear all of the views, and then when they decide, they move forward as a unified front—even though one or two of them may still think differently. That's important. Once you have your say, you don't try to tear it down afterward. A lot of organizations have managers who don't know when to stop and [therefore] create all kinds of chaos."

■ ■ ■

Like the previous generation, the new generation took the helm during a period of economic difficulty. In the late 1960s, the Seattle region was in the thralls of what locals remember as the "Boeing Bust," which was brought about when the federal government terminated funding for construction of a supersonic transport plane [SST], and Boeing abandoned the project. Coupled with a decreased demand for the new 747 jumbo jet, Boeing went into a tailspin, reducing its Seattle-area payroll from 104,000 to 40,000 by 1971. Unemployment shot up over 12 percent—the top rate in the United States and the highest of any major city since the Great Depression. So many people moved out of the region there eventually appeared a billboard that read (albeit ungramatically): "The last person leaving Seattle—turn out the lights."

The family received another blow when Everett Nordstrom collapsed and died while playing golf at the Seattle Golf Club on July 1, 1972, at the age of sixty-nine.

The Nordstrom family, which had cut its teeth on coping with the Great Depression, decided to take the offensive against the recession. Lloyd assembled Nordstrom sales associates, buyers, and department managers and told them to buy more merchandise and hire more people. "That's when Nordstrom grew to be the best," recalled Patrick Kennedy, the corporate merchandiser manager for men's shoes. "Our people have the experience of weathering storms. We don't get flustered. We go back to the basics. Fearful retailers make rash decisions, like getting rid of a lot of people and cutting expenses and amenities." The Nordstroms showed their faith in downtown Seattle by spending $7 million on a major remodeling of the flagship store, combining what were originally three separate buildings into one 245,000-square-foot building. When they opened the remodeled store at the end of 1973, the name was formally changed to Nordstrom, Incorporated.

Nordstrom was the largest-volume specialty fashion apparel store on the West Coast, with annual sales over $100 million, and was well on the way to becoming the Saks Fifth Avenue of the Pacific Northwest. With their state-of-the-art downtown flagship store as their retail laboratory, the Nordstroms were confident that their formula would travel well throughout the rest of the West Coast, if not the entire United States. In 1975, Nordstrom acquired three stores in Alaska from the Northern Commercial Company. The following year, Nordstrom created a new store concept that catered to younger customers. Called "Place Two," these stores were 15,000- to 20,000-square-foot spaces that stocked shoes, clothing, cosmetics, and accessories, and were often located in small college towns. (This division has since been phased out in favor of concentrating resources on the larger main-line stores.)

■ ■ ■

In 1975, Lloyd Nordstrom headed a group of Seattle investors who sought an expansion National Football League franchise for the city. For the Nordstrom family, "it was a civic venture," said Mike McCormack, a member of the Professional Football Hall of Fame, who became director of football operations for the Seahawks in 1982. "The local group needed a major player, so the Nordstrom family stepped up. They made a family decision for the good of the area. Not a lot of people realize the commitment they made when other people thought it was too expensive to do." The price tag was $16 million, which seems like an absolute bargain by today's standards. The NFL insisted that one person had to be the majority owner, but none of the Seattle investors had the required $8 million–plus. Lloyd convinced the NFL, particularly his friend, commissioner Pete Rozelle, to designate the Nordstrom *family* as the owner of 51 percent of the team. "Lloyd was aware of the fact that the if the league did well, it would bring Seattle along with it," Rozelle recalled.

Under the Nordstrom regime, the Seahawks became one of the most admired and best-run franchises in all of professional sports. They ran their football team as they ran their stores—decentralized. When McCormack joined the Seahawks in 1982, Elmer had taken over as managing partner from Herman Sarkowsky, a Seattle businessman and sportsman. "They felt they wanted to get a football man in the front office administration as a go-between for the coaching staff and the front office. Later, it was explained to me that it was the Nordstrom policy. John [who later succeeded Elmer as managing partner] told me many times that 'When we hire a merchandise manager we want someone who knows merchandising and we wanted a football person to run our football operations.'" At the time, that was a novel approach, according to McCormack, who said, "Eventually, thanks to the Nordstroms, putting football people in charge of football operations became in vogue" in the NFL.

"I have always said that ownership allows you to be successful," said McCormack. "In my eight years with the team, not once were we ever denied anything. We were given permission to run the club and keep the Nordstroms apprised; they didn't want any surprises. But at the same time, they wanted us to make good decisions. They gave us guidance and counsel. All I had to do was operate within their framework. I'm very proud of the fact that during our time in charge of the operation, we were the only ones who have ever been associated with the Seahawks to have a winning record." In 1983, the Seahawks were champions of the Western Division of the American Football Conference of the NFL—the only title in the team's history.

The Nordstroms exhibited the same consistency of approach to football that they have to retailing. "This was something that John and his whole family imparted to me," said McCormack. "The players want you to be consistent; if you are inconsistent, they have doubts in you. It's so important that employees know where they stand. There's not going to be one set of rules today and another tomorrow."

In 1988, the Nordstroms chose to concentrate their energies and their cash on their ambitious retail expansion. First they bought out the 49 percent interest of the five minority owners for $35 million, then sold the team for about $80 million in cash to Kenneth Behring, a California real estate developer. "They felt that the Nordstrom company needed the work of all of them, so they couldn't have the distraction of the football team," Pete Rozelle recalled. "I was very, very sorry about it. I understood their decision, but I still didn't like it. I really wanted them to stay in the league. I was particularly impressed with their togetherness. We've had many ownerships, where you get involved in litigations and so forth among the partnerships. There was never any friction with their ownership. As a family, they were always on the same page. You are always going to have trouble with a club somewhere along the line on some issues, but we never had one single bit of a problem with the Nordstroms."

■ Pointing to Mecca: The California Market

By 1977, with sales of almost $250 million, Nordstrom was the third-largest quality apparel specialty retailer in the United States behind only Saks Fifth Avenue and Lord & Taylor. "We think of ourselves as the Bloomingdale's of the West," Jim Nordstrom told *Forbes* in a 1978 feature story called "Bloomies in the Boonies." That same year, the Nordstroms made their most pivotal decision since acquiring Best's Apparel: expanding into California, where the Nordstrom name was barely known. "Never before had we devoted so much time and money in the planning of a new store because this was a totally new market for us and it was vital that we get a strong start," the Nordstroms said in the company's 1979 annual report to stockholders.

"California was going to be Mecca," recalled Betsy Sanders, the Nordstrom executive who was put in charge of the move. "It was fraught with challenge but it was exciting. There was no matrix, no plan, no instruction, which has always been how Nordstrom works. Except this was on a bigger scale than we normally did it. We invented this region as we went along." One of Sanders's first orders of business was to recruit people to work in the store. "No one had been hired with the exception of the shoe buyer. At first, we were told that we could not find anyone in southern California to give the kind of service that we had developed a reputation for. And if we did, it wouldn't matter because we would find no customers interested in us. We were virtually unknown in southern California. People would stand in the middle of the mall and look down towards our end and say, 'What's a Nordstein?' I heard that more than once. The only people who had heard of us were those who had lived in the Northwest, and they were crazy about the fact that we were coming."

To attract new employees, Nordstrom ran a clever newspaper advertisement with the headline, "Wanted: People Power," accompanied by copy that described the positive personal attributes that Nordstrom was looking for: "People who genuinely like people; who find satisfaction in helping others; in going out of their way to be of service." On the strength of that ad, there were over 1,500 applicants, all of whom were interviewed by Sanders and two assistants. In keeping with the Nordstrom policy of hiring from within, all of the new buyers for the California store were company veterans.

In May 1978, the company opened a 124,000-square-foot, three-level store at the South Coast Plaza shopping center in Costa Mesa. The new store boasted the biggest shoe department in the state of California—10,000 square feet for women's shoes, 3,000 for men's, and 2,500 for children's. As the doors of the store opened for the first time, employees lined up at the entrances and spontaneously began to applaud the shoppers as they entered. "Our people were simply overcome with excitement," said Betsy Sanders. This expression of appreciation quickly became a Nordstrom tradition at every new store opening, and continues to this day.

"We opened six weeks after Nieman-Marcus," Sanders recalled. "They were seven miles away, much heralded and highly anticipated. We were the also-rans. We had a hard time getting anyone to talk to us and generate interest in us." Nevertheless, the store became an instant success, and early on became the biggest-volume Nordstrom store. "The customers liked us, but our competitors waited for us to send everybody back to Seattle. They presumed we just brought in people for the opening and that it would then be back to business as usual. Well, it never turned into business as usual. Eventually, they began telling people in their training classes that they were going to have to start smiling and being nice to the customer because Nordstrom was coming and that's how Nordstrom sales people act. They never got the point that it wasn't an act."

The Costa Mesa store was followed a year and a half later by a second store at the Brea shopping center in Los Angeles County. Today, Nordstrom is the dominant fashion specialty retailer in California, generating sales of $1 billion from twenty-six full-line stores and five Nordstrom Rack clearance stores. (Rack stores sell merchandise originally stocked at regular Nordstrom stores as well as special purchases of end-of-the-season close-outs or over-run merchandise from other vendors, at 50 percent or more off the original price.)

Nordstrom benefited from the troubles that major department stores were having in the latter part of the 1980s, an era marked by retail-merger mania. In 1986, Campeau Corporation, headed by Canadian businessman Robert Campeau, paid a highly inflated price—$3.6 billion—for Allied Stores Corporation (which included Jordan Marsh, Sterns, and The Bon Marche) and less than two years later, acquired Federated Department Stores (which included Bloomingdale's, Abraham & Straus, Lazarus, Burdines, and Rich's) for an even more inflated $6.6 billion. Both deals were "leveraged buyouts," which were paid for mostly by high-interest "junk bonds." Faced with crushing interest costs and other problems, the Campeau empire collapsed. Thousands of retail jobs were eliminated and corporate expenses were slashed in order to pay off the massive debt.

By the end of 1995, Nordstrom was operating fifty-nine large specialty stores in Washington, Oregon, California, Utah, Alaska, Virginia, New Jersey, Illinois, Maryland, and Minnesota, five smaller specialty stores, thirteen Rack stores, and eleven leased shoe departments in the Liberty House department stores in Hawaii, proving that the Nordstrom way of doing business could be exported all over the country.

Key to the Nordstrom expansion strategy is to open stores in new markets "with all guns blazing," said Bruce Nordstrom. "I think we get off to a running start better than anybody. We say, 'let's be beautiful, let's be great, let's have a beautiful opening party and donate lots of money to the local charity.' We haven't made a cent yet, but we're going to do those things first." He believed that most retailers suffer from "myopic thinking" when planning a store. "They say, 'the store is 150,000 square feet, so we're going to do $25 million [in first year sales] in that store. That means we are going to buy X amount of inventory, we're going to hire X amount of people, and we're going to buy X amount of ads.' So when they do only $22 million, they say, 'that's pretty good; we're just about on budget.'" The Nordstrom approach "is a little more freewheeling than that. We enjoy a reputation. There is a curiosity in each new town that we go into. People want to see our store. When you open a store, it's so crucial that you don't disappoint. You want to impress."

Nordstrom gives the local store manager the autonomy "to hire a huge sales staff and to buy as much inventory for their departments as the shelves will hold," Bruce continued. "We will build up the crew so that those legions of people who pour in don't get disappointed. On that first day or first week or first month, you're going to do an abnormal amount of business. You're going to be exposed to an abnormal amount of people—particularly in our case. So, we have abnormally large staffs. We have a lot of our vendors come in and help us. We will transfer people in from other stores and help us. That's one of the benefits of a company like ours. A new store can find its level pretty quickly. After a month or two, as things settle down, we ask our managers to get things in line for normal business. We open a few stores that do $100 million a year in their first year. That's never been done by anybody."

■ Transferring the Culture

As previously mentioned, Nordstrom eschews the acquisition and conversion of other chains (or parts of chains) to Nordstrom stores—even though it takes more time to build, stock, and open a new Nordstrom store in a new market, establish the service-level consistency, and win over the consuming public. Because Nordstrom considers its culture the key element separating it from the competition, when the company expands to other regions, it relies on experienced, trailblazing "Nordies" to bring the culture with them to these new markets and to teach and inspire new employees in customer service the Nordstrom way. A case in point is the Tysons Corner, Virginia, store, which was the company's first East Coast retail enterprise. Months before the store opened in 1988, about ninety experienced Nordstrom department managers moved to Virginia from California, Washington, Oregon, Utah, and Alaska, and more than 300 veteran Nordstrom sales associates volunteered to relocate at their own expense. They were motivated by opportunities to move ahead in the company.

"It was exciting because we knew we were involved in something from the ground up," said Len Kuntz, one of those pioneers, who transferred to Tysons Corner as a men's wear buyer. "Having only one store in the region at that time, the buyers and merchandise managers were on the floor all the time, interacting with the sales people and the customers and getting involved in the community. That helped nail down our philosophies a lot quicker than anything else and gave the store a distinct personality." Still, Kuntz and others had a lot of convincing to do when recruiting new associates. "For a long time, a lot of people who started with us thought of us as just another department store. Their image of a department store was a place where you hang out for a while before you get a 'real' job. They thought of it in terms of being a clerk, as opposed to a salesperson involved in the business. They were used to just standing by a register and ringing up stuff when the customer brought it to them. We had a little bit of turnover there."

Since then, as Nordstrom has moved into other new markets, "we keep improving our ability to translate what we are as a company with the people that we bring," said Jack McMillan. "We can communicate who and what we are, and what we want to be; and then attract the kind of people that want to be on the team, to play retail the way we play it—as a profession that people can be really proud of."

Bruce Nordstrom concurred: "What I'm most proud of is that we have sustained and enlarged the culture that drives our company. I hope that this doesn't sound empty, but our service and the resulting reputation are better today than what they were when I was twenty-one years old. That says it all as far as I'm concerned. Does that mean we don't get complaints or that we don't do dumb things? No."

When Nordstrom opened its first Midwest store in the Oak Brook Mall in suburban Chicago, Bob Middlemas, who was named manager of the new store, was charged with putting his team together. "One of the beauties of our company is that I can call on a lot of people to help me," he said. "I went to every region of the company and talked to people who had sent me letters of interest in being part of the new Chicago team. From that group, I picked my core team, which consisted of about twenty people. Those folks hired people in different levels of management in our division. We came out with 100 seasoned Nordstrom employees, so we had a very solid foundation."

More than 4,000 people applied for some 600 positions. "This was during the Persian Gulf war. The economy was down. We were able to attract a lot of people from outside of retailing, who had heard about Nordstrom," recalled Middlemas. He and other Nordstrom veterans explained to the applicants how the company operates. Then each of them talked about their own careers and accomplishments at Nordstrom. As they spoke, "our people were so proud and appreciative of our company that they would start to cry. There were people in the audience, who were so touched by this that *they* were crying along with them."

Middlemas and the other Nordstrom veterans soon discovered that virtually all of the people they hired had not been allowed to make decisions at their previous jobs, where they had been just "worker bees," said Middlemas. "We told them that we simplify what we are trying to accomplish. We said, *'You will never be criticized for doing too much for a customer, you will only be criticized for doing too little. If you're ever in doubt as to what to do in a situation, always make a decision that favors the customer before the company.'* It took about six months for people to be comfortable with making their own decisions, but it has paid a huge dividend to us as we continue to grow our customer base in this market."

True to form, Nordstrom didn't want to offend the people they didn't hire. So managers were encouraged to call back all applicants who didn't get jobs and thank them for their time. Middlemas explained: "We wanted them to become Nordstrom customers."

It didn't take long for people on the East Coast to grasp Nordstrom's commitment to satisfying the customer. There were, however, some humorous incidents. On the first day Tysons Corner was open for business, sales associate Annette Armony put together an outfit for a woman shopping for a gift for her granddaughter. Armony put the outfit in a gift box and wrapped it with a bow. Suddenly, the customer became indignant. She vociferously declared that she had no intention of paying the extra money for the box or the bow. "Out of the corner of my eye, I see Bruce Nordstrom walking down the aisle," recalled Armony. "I'm thinking, 'Oh, no.'" Armony tried to explain to the agitated customer that the box and bow were *on Nordstrom*. When she finally comprehended, she reversed herself and kept repeating, "I can't believe this! I can't believe this!" Bruce Nordstrom asked Armony if everything was okay. She explained the situation. "Mr. Bruce told the customer, 'Yes, it's complimentary. No problem.' When the lady left the store, she was on cloud nine."

With such small but compelling touches, Nordstrom changed the customer service attitude of the competition. Co-chairman John Nordstrom noted that when he visits new stores that are about to open, he likes to talk to the new associates about where they previously worked and what they knew about Nordstrom prior to joining the company. Invariably, they tell of their previous employers continually bringing up Nordstrom's customer service. "It's so dumb for those other companies to do that," said John Nordstrom. "They have to do their own thing. Why do they talk about us?"

Art Langelotti, a men's wear salesman for Nordstrom at Garden State Plaza in Paramus, noted that, not long after Nordstrom opened in the mall, his wife began getting frequent follow-up phone calls and reminders of upcoming sales from a sales associate at Macy's, another anchor tenant in the mall. When Langelotti's wife asked the Macy's employee why she was so diligent, she answered that she was developing her customer-service habits because "I'm waiting to be hired by Nordstrom." Although she was working for the competition, she was already practicing customer service the Nordstrom way.

When Van Mensah, who now sells men's suits at Nordstrom's Pentagon City, Virginia, store, was working at Woodward & Lothrop, a Washington, D.C., department store, he and other Woodward & Lothrop employees were shown an instructional video on how Nordstrom operates. The video was part of a program to get employees to act more like Nordstrom employees. "That was the first time I had heard about Nordstrom," Mensah recalled. After the seminar, "we had to assess how we felt about the program. I told my boss that the program would not work because the Woodward & Lothrop culture was so different from Nordstrom. You couldn't just pick up some aspects of one company's culture and try to impose it on another's. My prediction was true."

Nordstrom became such a feared competitor that Woodward & Lothrop tried to keep the Annapolis Mall in Maryland from expanding after it had been passed over as an anchor store by the developer, who chose Nordstrom. Although Woodies cited environmental and traffic concerns as the reasons for its opposition, the general opinion was that its displeasure was based on competitive considerations—for twenty-eight years, the D.C. retailer had a store in another mall, about half a mile away. The legal appeal ultimately was dropped because it was filed four days after the deadline. (Woodward & Lothrop filed for Chapter 11 bankruptcy protection in 1994.)

When Nordstrom's Annapolis Mall store opened in March 1994, the executives who ran the Capital Region (of which this store would be a part) decided on their own to use the opportunity to introduce itself to the community in a special way. In the past, when Nordstrom opened a new store, part of its strategy was to put on a lavish formal opening party that helped raise hundreds of thousands of dollars for a local charity, so that people would see that Nordstrom puts money into a community before it rings up its first sale. The people at Nordstrom's Annapolis store used a more grass-roots approach. More than 250 of them took part in a "Community Service Day" with six United Way organizations—TreeMendous Maryland, the Annapolis Boys & Girls Club, Helping Hand, Arundel Lodge, YMCA, and the Annapolis Youth Services Bureau. Their tasks ranged from preparing seedling trees for planting to refurbishing and painting emergency shelters and senior housing.

"I don't know who benefited more—our employees or the community," recalled Martha S. Wikstrom, Nordstrom Capital Region general manager. "It speaks to what we feel. When we go into a city as a big corporation, we want to be their hometown store. Our directives don't come from Seattle, Washington; our directives come from the customers who live in that community. So, our efforts need to be towards those people. This was a project of the nineties. People are looking less to big parties and more to individual efforts that mean something. You can always write a check."

The competitors no longer underestimate Nordstrom. In 1990, when Nordstrom opened its store in Paramus, Macy's placed a full-page ad in the *New York Times,* hailing its competitor from Seattle. The ad pictured a toddler arranging blocks that spelled out Macy's and Nordstrom. Below, in large type, the copy read: "Macy's welcomes the new kid on the block." But when Macy's fell into Chapter Eleven bankruptcy in 1993 and was forced to slash expenses and squeeze its staff, Macy's management apparently decided to leave customer service to "the new kid on the block." In a story published in the March 17, 1994, issue of *Women's Wear Daily,* an unnamed Macy's executive conceded, "We'll never be Nordstrom. Customer's don't expect it."

KEYS TO SUCCESS

Trained from the sales floor as shoe salesmen, the third generation of Nordstroms—Bruce, John, and Jim Nordstrom, and Jack McMillan—were literally and figuratively raised kneeling in front of the customer, whom they acknowledged as the primary source of their livelihood. They have emulated their fathers' decision-by-consensus philosophy and, in the process, built the company into what it is today.

- They have created, through expansion, a fast career track for energetic, entrepreneurial people, who are rewarded for their performance with advancement and increased responsibility. Promoting from within is an essential ingredient in Nordstrom's success.
- Beginning in the late 1960s, the Nordstroms established an open career path for women. Today, almost 40 percent of company officers and 66 percent of store managers are female.
- Store managers have the autonomy to hire a huge sales staff and to buy as much inventory for their departments as the shelves will hold. When entering a new community, the company introduces itself with an opening party that generates hundreds of thousands of dollars for a local charity.
- A distinctive culture separates Nordstrom from the competition. When the company expands to other regions, it dispatches an advanced force of veteran "Nordies" who carry the culture with them and impart it to new employees. These trailblazers are motivated by opportunities for advancement.
- Nordstrom doesn't acquire other chains (or parts of chains) and convert them to Nordstrom stores because it is too difficult for those employees to break old habits.
- Employees are instructed to always make a decision that favors the customer before the company. They are never criticized for doing too much for a customer; they are criticized for doing too little.

4 The Nordstrom Culture

Setting Employees Free

One day, Van Mensah, a men's-clothing sales associate at Nordstrom's Pentagon City, Virginia, store, received a disturbing letter from one of his better customers, an executive with a well-known Swedish-based manufacturer. The gentleman had recently purchased some $2,000 worth of shirts and ties from Mensah, and when he mistakenly washed the shirts in hot water, they all shrunk. He was not writing to complain (he readily conceded the mistake was his), but to ask Mensah's professional advice on how he should deal with his predicament.

Mensah immediately put a telephone call through to Sweden, and told the customer that he would replace those shirts with new ones at no charge. He asked the customer to mail the other shirts back to Nordstrom—at Nordstrom's expense. "I didn't have to ask for anyone's permission to do what I did for that customer," said Mensah, a native of Ghana, who holds a Masters of Business Administration from Northeastern University in Boston. "Nordstrom would rather leave it up to me to decide what's best."

97

Empowering the people on the sales floor with the freedom to accept returned merchandise (even when the damage was done by the customer) is the most noticeable illustration of the Nordstrom culture because it is the one that affects the public.

Nordstrom is informally organized as an "inverted pyramid" (see illustration below), with the top position occupied by the customers, followed in descending order by salespeople; department managers; store managers, buyers, merchandise managers, regional managers, general managers; co-presidents Raymond A. Johnson and

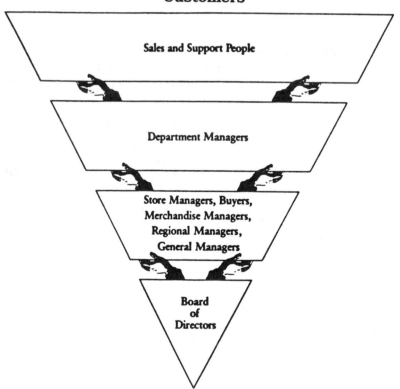

Customers

Sales and Support People

Department Managers

Store Managers, Buyers,
Merchandise Managers,
Regional Managers,
General Managers

Board
of
Directors

John J. Whitacre, directors, and, at the bottom, the co-chairmen John, Bruce, and James Nordstrom and Jack McMillan. The inverted pyramid was born in the early 1970s, when Nordstrom made its initial public offering of stock. A stock analyst asked the company for its organizational chart. To his surprise, none existed. Somebody suggested that "we take a pyramid and flip it upside down," recalled John Nordstrom. What sets Nordstrom apart is that, from department manager to co-chairman, all tiers of the inverted pyramid work to support the sales staff, not the other way around. "The only thing we have going for us is the way we take care of our customers," explained Johnson, "and the people who take care of the customers are on the floor."

Nordstrom managers continually reinforce the message that it has confidence in the ability of its people to make good choices. "So many things are common sense," said Len Kuntz, a former manager of the Pentagon City store, who is now corporate sales promotion director. "If you give people leeway and credit, most of the time they're going to do the right thing." And if you do the wrong thing, said Kazumi Ohara, who manages Chanel Accessories in the downtown Seattle store, "you say you're sorry and start all over again."

"People will work hard," said Jim Nordstrom, "when they are given the freedom to do the job the way they think it should be done, when they treat customers the way they like to be treated. When you take away their incentive and start giving them rules, boom, you've killed their creativity." Nordstrom director Ann D. McLaughlin, former U.S. Secretary of Labor, said she periodically reminds the other corporate boards that she serves on about Nordstrom's philosophy of not forcing the customer to abide by a lot of corporate regulations. "The idea is for us to adapt to the customer, to make the system work for them; not the other way around. The customer is the one who drives the business. How many times have you had a store tell you, 'No, you can't do that'?" said McLaughlin, who also serves on the board of, among others, General Motors Corporation, Host Marriott Corporation, Kellogg Company, and AMR Corporation and its subsidiary American Airlines.

Giving salespeople and managers at all levels a wide range of operational and bottom-line responsibility (such as controlling costs), without shackling them with lots of bureaucratic guidelines, which get in the way of serving the customer, allows Nordstrom people to operate like entrepreneurial shopkeepers rather than blocks in a retailing monolith. "We can move on a dime and effect things quickly," said Martha S. "Marty" Wikstrom, vice-president and general manager of Nordstrom's Capital region, a five-store group in the Washington, D.C./Maryland area. "Bureaucracies are too cumbersome to get anything accomplished."

Again, the most obvious example is the return policy, which is virtually an unconditional, money-back guarantee. (There are some exceptions, due to public health laws, in certain departments.) If customers aren't completely satisfied with their purchase, for whatever reason, the store takes it back, no questions asked. Bruce Nordstrom tells sales people, "If a customer came into the store with a pair of five-year-old shoes and complained that the shoes were worn out and wanted her money back, you have the right to use your best judgment to give my money away. As a matter of fact, I *order* you to give my money away."

Doesn't that unconditional policy invite abuse? Sure it does, but central to the Nordstrom philosophy is a desire not to punish the many for the dishonesty of a few. Nordstrom wants to keep happy "the 98 percent of the people who are honest; that's who we cater to," said Deborah Kirsch, who sells women's shoes at the Oak Brook

Mall store. "Jim Nordstrom tells us that we have the right to tell the customer, '*I* guarantee [the return]. The company may not guarantee it, but *I* do.' That's a great selling tool."

Which is not to say that returns are not often frustrating for Nordstrom salespeople. "You have that customer who 'borrows' [a dress] for a couple of years and then returns it," said Joyce Johnson, who sells couture women's apparel in the Collectors department of the Nordstrom store in Corte Madera, a suburb of San Francisco. "But you have to realize that returns are part of the game. You have to learn that even when you take back your returns, you smile, because those people will come back to you."

That's exactly what Everett, Elmer, and Lloyd Nordstrom had in mind when they established this generous warranty back when Nordstrom was a two-store operation. The brothers dreaded having to deal with obviously outrageous or unreasonable returns, so, they reckoned, if they could pass off the responsibilities for the adjustments and complaints, the business would be more personally enjoyable. "We decided to let the clerks make the adjustments, so they would be the fair-haired boys," recalled Elmer. "We told them, 'If the customer is not pleased, she can come to us and we'll give her what she wants anyway.'" The Nordstroms tracked the costs of the return policy for the first year and found they could afford to maintain it. Plus, in a world where most retailers made returns an ordeal, Nordstrom made the experience as painless as possible, which generated priceless word-of-mouth advertising. It still does.

"The return policy is one of the most important things about shopping at Nordstrom," said customer Vicky LaGrone. "If I bring something home and I try it on and don't like it, I can return it just as quickly as I took it out of the store. There's no hassle."

For many years, LaGrone was a regular customer of Patrice Nagasawa, who sells fashion-forward designer women's apparel in the Savvy Department of Nordstrom's store in the Bellevue Square shopping center in suburban Seattle. When LaGrone moved to Texas, she continued to be a customer—via mail—of Nagasawa.

"Just because there's not a Nordstrom store where you live doesn't mean you can't keep shopping at Nordstrom," quipped Nagasawa.

Ann McLaughlin described the return policy as emblematic of Nordstrom's *authenticity.* "They are authentic in that they say they're going to do something and they do it. They are authentic in how they represent themselves as a store to the customer," said McLaughlin, who is president of the Federal City Council of Washington, D.C., and vice-chairman of The Aspen Institute. While shopping at Nordstrom, McLaughlin once overheard a young woman in her twenties tell her mother she was going to buy both pairs of shoes she was trying on. "The young woman said, 'I really like them both, but if I decide when I get home that I don't want one, I know that I can always bring it back.' I don't know how many times I've heard similar comments. That's the authenticity of Nordstrom living up to their commitment on their return policy. It emanates from their understanding of the customer."

Nordstrom also gives salespeople the freedom to sell an item at a lower price, if necessary, in order to match the competition. "If you tell people they can't meet the competitor's price, you are telling them to take care of *me*," said Jim Nordstrom, "not the customer. We tell them, 'Don't bother calling your manager. Just meet the price.'"

But some people can't handle all that freedom. Co-president John Whitacre recalled that at one training session prior to the opening of Nordstrom's first East Coast store at Tysons Corner, Maryland, a new employee admitted that she would have problems with such a freewheeling atmosphere. Structure was what she was after. "Tell me exactly what you want me to do," she implored Whitacre, "and I promise I'll do it *that* way."

■ Tearing Down Barriers

Once a salesperson has established a rapport with a customer and helped put together the right look, she wants to make sure all of the customer's needs are met in order to complete the package. So Nordstrom frees salespeople to sell merchandise to their customers in any department throughout the store. "Nordstrom salespeople are saying, 'I'm a customer-oriented service person. You are looking for something, and I'm determined I'm going to find it, because somewhere Nordstrom has it,'" observed Donald Petersen, the retired chairman of Ford. Petersen said his wife, Jody, experienced this behavior firsthand at Nordstrom's downtown Seattle store. "She wasn't feeling much like shopping and was certain it was the wrong time of year for what she was looking for," Petersen recalled. "A woman in the St. John boutique said she could find the things my wife was looking for elsewhere in the store. Two hours later, Jody had purchased all kinds of things from other departments in the store."

Of course, the freedom to sell throughout the store gives go-go salespeople greater opportunity for higher sales. Patrice Nagasawa considered her business "one-stop shopping. If it's not nailed down, I'll find it for the customer. A customer wanted a case of hangers, so I ordered them from our distribution center. Another customer wanted to buy some of our long, plastic garment bags. I don't make commission on those things, but it's part of the service I provide."

Nordstrom's commitment to one-person continuity of service has inspired at least one company, Burlington Northern Railroad, to create a new customer service position for the railroad—account leader. This position is filled by a logistics expert, who is given total responsibility for the relationship between Burlington Northern and the shipper/customer. Instead of working out of the railroad's headquarters, account leaders are stationed in the offices of their customers, making them part of the customers' logistics team. "As a result, instead of customers having to talk to six, eight, or ten people within our company to find out about pricing, car availability, arrival time, and billing, they need only talk to that one person, who can solve all of their problems," said Jerry Grinstein, chairman and chief executive officer of Burlington Northern Railroad, and a twenty-year Nordstrom customer. Burlington Northern account leaders are charged with finding creative solutions for problems, such as accommodating changes in a customer's business or offering other transportation alternatives. "Rather than focusing on the difficulty of delivering the product or on the costs that we have to control, this broader and more significant service forces us to *think like the customer*," said Grinstein, "and enables us to guarantee the customer that they will get the service that we commit to provide."

■ Managing

The next level of the inverted pyramid is represented by department managers. Like everyone else at Nordstrom, department managers begin their careers as salespeople in order to learn what's required to take care of the customer. "Starting on the sales floor sends the signal from management that it values that role more than almost anything. All up and down the organization, people appreciate the importance of this function and what it means for everything else in the organization. It's critical," said Dr. Alfred E. Osborne, Jr., a Nordstrom director, director of the Entrepreneurial Studies Center, and an associate professor of business economics at the John E. Anderson Graduate School of Management, University of California, Los Angeles. The Nordstrom family's own sales experiences fostered an appreciation for what sales associates go through and for what it takes to satisfy the customer. As they readily concede, when they were young sales associates and didn't have what the customer asked for, they weren't good enough salespeople to be able to switch the customer to another item.

Managers are encouraged to have a feeling of ownership about their department. They are responsible for hiring (the personnel department does little recruitment), firing, scheduling, training, coaching, nurturing, encouraging, and evaluating their sales team. Rather than sit behind a desk, Nordstrom managers, like the proprietors of small boutiques, are expected to spend some of their time on the selling floor, interacting with the customers and the sales staff. They are paid a salary plus commission on any sales they make, and are eligible for a bonus tied to percentage increases in sales over the previous year. "It doesn't matter what the department manager does as much as what everybody else is doing," said Len Kuntz, who characterized the role of department manager as "probably the hardest job in our company. You have to have a lot of balls in the air." Yet department manager has been his favorite post at Nordstrom because, "You can teach people and build strong teams. The only difference between stores is the people they have."

The store manager's primary responsibility is to set the tone for what happens on the sales floor. "I spent 75 percent of my time on the sales floor interacting with the managers, the salespeople, and the customers," said Kuntz. "When customers looked lost, I offered them directions. When your people see you doing that, they realize that's the focus of the company. Much of what happens in this company is environmental. You absorb it by watching and seeing the focus and priorities, and it snowballs."

Jammie Baugh, executive vice-president and general manager of Nordstrom's southern California region, constantly cautions store managers not to micromanage because "that will shift the accountability away from the salesperson and you end up creating foot soldiers instead of lieutenants. When we are at our best, our frontline people are lieutenants because they control the business. Our competition has foot soldiers on the front line and lieutenants in the back." When Nordstrom's business in California went into a three-year slump because of that state's near-depression economy, it was tempting for management to want to take back some of the power. "We were guilty of that," Baugh conceded. "These tough economic times in California went on for much longer than anyone expected. But, as I learned from the Nordstrom family— Mr. Jim especially—you've got to keep your message simple. We need to *manage the expectation; not the people.* We were guilty of managing the people. You absolutely have to fight that urge all the time. We had to let it be the salesperson's deal."

Wikstrom, manager of the Capital region, noted that some new salespeople have difficulty adjusting to the intimate involvement of their managers. "One of our store managers had a woman on her staff who had previously worked for a company where the only time she ever saw her manager on the floor was when there was a complete disaster. So, when she came to work at Nordstrom, every time the store manager came on the floor, she would flinch and get very nervous. Finally, she asked the store manager, 'What's the hitch? Every time you come out on the floor, you're so nice.'"

■ Decentralized Buying

Because Nordstrom is decentralized, buyers in each region are more attuned to what the customers in their areas want, which, Nordstrom believes, is the number one customer service. Buyers, who are responsible for a relatively small group of stores, are given the freedom to acquire merchandise that reflects local lifestyles and tastes. For example, apparel buyers at Nordstrom's store in the Mall of America in Bloomington, Minnesota, procure more winter clothes than their counterparts in southern California.

Nordstrom buyers are responsible for just a few stores, so they can afford to take a chance on a unique, fashion-forward item without jeopardizing the company's bottom line. "If you're buying for seventy stores and you make a mistake, you're going to get killed. If you're buying for four, it's a small problem," said Jim Nordstrom. He felt that the competition's centralized buying systems make little sense and save little money, although he conceded, "it sure seems easier to get your arms around."

Buyers, many of whom also manage their own departments, receive their feedback directly from the salespeople and the customers because they are encouraged to spend several hours a week on the sales floor. "Interacting with the customer is so powerful," said Kuntz. "Computer spreadsheets can tell you what's selling, but they can't tell you what you're *not* selling because you don't have it in stock. The best buyers in our company are good listeners."

Jim Nordstrom said that "When we go into a new market, our first buy is our worst" because buyers have not gotten feedback from the customer. Once they get that response, buyers can quickly adjust when a particular line, look, or price point is not selling. For example, when Nordstrom opened its Pentagon City store, it stocked couture gowns, but soon discovered that they didn't have a sufficient number of couture customers. The department was eliminated and the space was filled by larger-sized dresses, which became one of that store's biggest departments.

Customers appreciate being able to talk directly with a manager or a buyer, said shoe salesperson Deborah Kirsch. If a customer wants to know when a particular shoe will be in stock, "I can turn to the buyer or manager and get the answer immediately. I don't have to say, 'Sorry, Ma'm, I'll need to take your name and number and get back to you.' I can give her an answer right away."

Nordstrom also encourages its vendors, particularly in footwear, to interact with Nordstrom customers. The company requires footwear sales representatives to call on each store in their territory and to work on the floor during store sale events, where they can earn the same commission rate as other Nordstrom footwear salespeople.

Nordstrom does have some centralized buying, particularly for imports and merchandise not available locally. On the other hand, footwear, which is the most individual of product categories, represents Nordstrom's quintessential decentralized department; every store has its own shoe-buying staff.

Still, Nordstrom's system is not perfect. Nordstrom occasionally finds itself stuck with bloated inventories, which means that buyers have to sharply mark down the price of merchandise in order to meet sales-volume goals. That strategy results in lower profits and grumpy stock analysts. But the company generally rights itself by the next quarter. Inventory that doesn't sell is quickly moved to other Nordstrom stores and/or the Nordstrom Rack clearance stores. But even when buyers make mistakes,

Nordstrom resists taking more direct central control over the buys. "That's not in our debate at all, just because that's the way we were raised," said Bruce Nordstrom. "I think there is something great about seeing a young buyer get a concept of a season—whether it be a color or a silhouette—that may be a little different from what *Women's Wear Daily* is talking about. She gives it a personal twist for that one department in that one store or state or region and, all of a sudden, you have a result that is 5 percent better than you're competitors. That's terrific."

Nordstrom's decentralized buying structure can be frustrating for manufacturers' sales representatives, who have to court so many Nordstrom buyers. "With us, they have to come to the state of Washington, Oregon, northern California, and so forth to make their pitch," said Bruce Nordstrom. On the other hand, decentralized buying gives a small, new vendor with a good idea "a chance to get his foot in the door in any one region." If the product sells, "we soon let our other buyers know about it. Then the next season, the vendor can gear up intelligently" to sell to other Nordstrom divisions. By contrast, Dillard's Department Stores has a very centralized organization, with a narrow core group of vendors that are connected electronically to Dillard's through bar coding. "I think that's great and it's obviously successful for them," said Bruce Nordstrom. "But there's no way that the next Anne Kleins and Calvin Kleins and Ralph Laurens, in their infancy, can get their foot in the door."

Nevertheless, Nordstrom has been forced to modify its fabled decentralized buying structure because too many inexperienced buyers were making too many costly mistakes. "Our [buyers] are given the most freedom [in retailing]; sometimes that freedom hasn't been used as judiciously as we think it should," said Bruce Nordstrom. "Giving a young man or woman free rein to do whatever they want, turned into a need to be different." That democratic approach "served us well in the eighties, when our [high volume] selling overcame buying mistakes. While we want to be decentralized, we can't give every rookie veto power on every issue."

Consequently, Nordstrom is delegating 80 percent of the final buying decisions in a particular category to a few experienced "lead buyers," who can negotiate with the vendor for large quantities of merchandise, so that Nordstrom can take advantage of its purchasing power. Lead buyers don't necessarily make all of the buy, but they are designated as the voice of the company in the marketplace. Nordstrom has always had lead buyers for footwear, which, as the oldest and most successful division, is where the Nordstrom culture is most deeply ingrained. Lead buying is more difficult in apparel, where inventory is sold and replaced much faster. Like other retailers, Nordstrom is cutting back on expensive buying trips because it prefers buyers to get their information firsthand by spending time on the selling floor. "The more time you can spend listening to your salespeople and your customers, the better equipped you will be to buy for those customers," said Jack McMillan. "Buyers don't need to spend so much time in the market talking to vendors."

At Nordstrom, empowerment for getting the right merchandise in the store begins not in the buying office, but on the floor—at the point of the sale. Nordstrom encourages salespeople to take the entrepreneurial initiative by giving their manager and buyer input on fashion direction, styles, quantities, sizes, and colors of the merchandise carried in their department. "If I see something that's hot, I'm going to ask our buyer to go for it," said David Butler, who sells women's shoes at the Tacoma store. "I give vendors feedback, too." Joe Dover, a men's shoe salesman at the Bellevue Square store, said, "My merchandiser,

Pat Kennedy, tells us that if the buyers don't see [our point], we should get in their face until they do." Leslie Kaufman, who sells men's clothing at the Westside store in Los Angeles, sometimes accompanies her buyer to New York in order provide a salesperson's perspective on the development of a special line of men's clothing.

Nordstrom believes that sharing responsibility and rewarding communication promotes loyalty, teamwork, and, perhaps most importantly, enthusiasm for the job. "There's nothing more demoralizing for a salesperson than to not be able to satisfy the customer," said Jim Nordstrom. "Our number-one responsibility to our sales associates is to have the products that the customers want when the customers come into the store. You can have all the pep rallies in the world, but the best motivation is stocking the right item in the right size at the right price."

Bob Middlemas, the general manager for the Midwest region, learned that lesson early in his career, when he was a men's tailored-clothing buyer in Nordstrom's Oregon region. Middlemas's merchandise manager was on sick leave and he filled in for several weeks. "One day, I'm sitting at my desk and I get a phone call from John Nordstrom.' That got my attention," Middlemas recalled. "He said, 'Bob, I was out visiting your region the last few days. I went to the men's furnishings department of your Clackamas Town Center store and I noticed that you didn't have any 17½, 35-inch white shirts. And your tall-men's tie selection looks very, very weak, considering what a trend that is in our men's furnishings business right now. Could you check on that and get back to me?'"

Middlemas learned that the distribution center was out of size 17½, 35-inch white shirts, but a new delivery was expected in a couple of weeks. The neckwear manufacturer said that the tall-men's ties were on their way to the distribution center and would be in the stores in a few days. Middlemas felt proud of himself "because I thought I had done my job. I called Mr. John back and said, "I got the answers you were looking for." Middlemas's explanation was met with silence on the other end of the phone. Finally, John Nordstrom replied: "Bob, you didn't understand my question. I didn't ask you *where* they were. I asked you *why* we didn't have them." The point, Middlemas realized, "was that I should figure out a way to solve the problem. If we don't have the stock, we should get it from one of our vendors so we don't walk [lose] a customer on a thirty-five-dollar dress shirt. Because if we walk him on the dress shirt, we're not going to sell him the shoes or the tie or the belt and he's going to be disappointed in our company."

Everett Nordstrom once gave one of his shoe buyers a similar lesson. When Everett asked the buyer why a size 7B in a certain style was not in stock, the buyer replied that it was on order. Everett asked for a copy of the order sheet. He folded it up, put it in a shoe box and placed the box on a shelf in the stockroom. "Now," he told the buyer, "when the customer for that size 7B comes into the store, tell her to try that order on."

Even as it grows, Nordstrom continues to strive "to put as much responsibility as possible into the hands of as many people as possible," said Bruce Nordstrom. "That's the only way to give the culture a chance to progress. Otherwise, it can't be done. With 35,000 employees, spread out over 3,000 miles, if you were dependent on Bruce or John or Jim Nordstrom, you couldn't do it. We keep pushing the power down to the sales floor. Human nature being what it is, there's no question that if you are in an ivory tower, sitting at a desk behind your computer and your reports, you'll say, 'I'm scared of the decisions they're going to make down on the floor.' I sometimes sit in my office here and wring my hands, but I know that in the long run, [our way] is better. I think I'm a good shoe-man. I think with a little crash course, I could be a good shoe buyer today. But there's no way I should be telling these folks what colors to buy, what heel heights to buy, what patterns to buy because I don't know enough about it. I'm not talking to those customers every day. If that confidence in the individual is repeated over and over and over again, it creates power there. This isn't a real scientific business. If we could harness peoples' good will, energy, and ideas and have it all go in one direction, then it would have to be successful."

■ Commissions

The Nordstrom system is entrepreneurial. Ever since the early 1950s, when Nordstrom sold only shoes, employee compensation has been based on commissions on net sales. The brothers knew the best way to attract and retain good people—self-starters who don't require a lot of supervision—was by paying them according to their ability. Commission sales and bonuses "gave them added incentive to work harder, and by working harder, they were often able to build a loyal customer following," Elmer Nordstrom wrote in *A Winning Team*, the privately published family history. In the 1960s, Nordstrom made one of its most important strategic moves when it became the nation's first apparel retailer to pay a meaningful sales commission. Eventually, Seattle became the first city in the United States where every major department and specialty chain had a system of commission selling.

Today, the standard commission on apparel sales at Nordstrom is 6.75 percent, 8.25 percent for men's shoes, 9 to 10 percent for women's shoes, and 13 percent for children's shoes. (These rates may vary slightly, according to what area of the country a store is located.)

Each salesperson has a designated draw, which is determined by dividing the commission percentage by a designated hourly rate. That rate varies, depending upon the competitive rates in each region. (At Nordstrom, the top range is from $9.50 to $11.00 per hour.) The amount of the draw varies with each department. In men's sportswear, for example, the 6.75 percent commission rate divided into an hourly wage rate of $9.50, equals $140.74 in sales per hour, which is Nordstrom's minimum hourly sales target for that specific department. At the end of each pay period, sales-per-hour performance is calculated by taking the net dollar volume of items sold, subtracting returns, and dividing that figure by the number of hours worked. For example, a salesperson rings up $22,000 in sales in an 80-hour pay period. Subtract $2,000 in returns, for net total sales of $20,000, or $250 per hour. That salesperson's commission for the pay period is 6.75 percent of $20,000, or $1,350.

If salespeople aren't making enough in commissions to cover their draw, then Nordstrom makes up the difference between commissions earned and their hourly rate. Employees who fail to regularly exceed their draw are targeted for special coaching by their department manager. If it doesn't appear that a career in sales is for them, they are either assigned to a nonsales area or are let go.

"When you have star salespeople, they ought to get paid like stars because they earn it," said Bruce Nordstrom. One of those stars is Leslie Kaufman of the Westside store who has been Nordstrom's top salesperson over the past three years. She racks up well over $1 million in sales every year, and in 1992 was featured in *USA Today* as one of the country's top retail salespeople. "The only way you become more successful is to sell more and develop more customers to buy more," said Kaufman. "If I were being paid only at an hourly rate, I don't think I'd be as motivated as I am. Knowing that my commission reflects how hard I work, it instills a different kind of drive in me. Nordstrom allows me to grow based on what I produce. The more you put into it, the more you're going to get out of it. It's easy to perform well for a day, a week, even a month. The key is to perform well year after year. That takes commitment and consistency."

Commissions-as-motivation caught the interest of other retailers, such as Macy's and May Department Stores Company, which restructured their compensation system by paying commission sales and instituting other incentives, such as stock options, non-stock performance plans linked to specific targets of return on capital, or earnings per share. When Nordstrom announced its expansion to the East Coast, retailers in Washington, D.C., didn't wait for Nordstrom to open its store at Tysons Corner. Bloomingdale's, for example, immediately expanded straight commissions or salary-plus-commissions to all departments at its D.C.-area stores. (Commissions previously had been paid only in the men's suits, designer dresses, shoes, rugs, and furniture departments.)

But commission selling by itself is not enough to guarantee customer service or motivate people. Again, if the store does not have the right item in stock at the right size at the right price, the commission system is an expensive indulgence. According to *Women's Wear Daily,* converting to commission selling can drive selling costs from 7 percent of a department store's overall volume to 10 percent in the first year, and increase costs by $700,000 to $1 million per store. In the late 1980s, Carter Hawley Hale Stores invested more than $30 million in its commission program but failed to realize any extraordinary productivity gains, and continued to lose market share to Nordstrom.

While other big retailers put a lot of their money into advertising, Nordstrom prefers to expend it on selling costs—the wages, commissions, and benefits for the many people on the floor—which represent the company's biggest business expense. The company provides sales associates with free thank-you notes (sent out to customers as a follow-up after the sale) and postcards (to alert customers to new merchandise, upcoming sales, or special events), as well as address labels, postage, and the use of the in-store word processing department, which creates personalized notes for each customer and maintains a customer list for every associate. "Nordstrom encourages sales associates to use these resources because that's what's going to make money for us and for the company," said Van Mensah.

These services can be costly when you have go-getters like Mensah or David Butler, who sells women's shoes in the Tacoma store, and has a mailing list of almost 2,000 customers. But Butler sells almost a million dollars worth of merchandise every year, which justifies the expense. That's part of the Nordstrom philosophy: *sales associates warrant their higher costs by generating more business than the competition.* Nordstrom believes that the best measure of its philosophy is sales-per-square-foot of selling space. A comparison illustrates this point: the May Department Stores Company, which is highly regarded by retail analysts for its ability to squeeze its operating costs, can barely muster $150 a square foot in sales, compared to Nordstrom's $400 a square foot. The only way stores can afford to pay commissions is by generating high sales volume. Once a store reaches the sales plateau where it can cover its fixed selling costs (including commissions), it can make a lot of money.

But even Nordstrom has found that sometimes commission selling doesn't work, and can, in fact, cause more problems than it solves. "When we entered Alaska, we instituted our policy in stores we took over. We didn't just lose the salespeople; we lost everybody, either in body or emotionally," Jim Nordstrom told *Women's Wear Daily.* "You have some people who just don't want to be in a pressurized selling environment. . . . When you have a corporate culture in place, it's hard to change the game. We have seen a lot of companies going after commission selling, but after a while, it peters out." The difference is that at Nordstrom, commission selling and goal setting—whether one likes them or not—are woven into the fabric of the company, rather than instituted by an outside customer service consultant or an edict from on high.

Some might feel that there is a dichotomy between customer service and commission sales. It's true that, in many cases, salespeople are happy to get the sale and are even happier to move on to another customer. They don't see themselves in a long-term relationship with a customer because they don't see themselves in a long-term relationship with their job. In 1992, Sears had to eliminate sales incentives for its auto center employees after they were found to have overcharged customers and pushed them into buying unneeded products and services. But at Nordstrom, top sales people argue that because their compensation is linked to satisfying the customer, it's in their best interest to act responsibly. "If I take care of the customer, the dollars will follow," said Patrice Nagasawa. "But you can't look at the customers with dollar signs in your eyes. With our liberal return policy, if people aren't happy with what they've purchased, it's going to come right back in your face, and that's not going to make anybody happy. It wastes their time and my time. A happy customer will refer me to her friends. She won't do that for someone she feels doesn't have her best interests at heart."

■ Motivation and Rewards

Like competitive athletes, Nordstrom salespeople are motivated in a variety of ways to give extraordinary service because extraordinary service produces extraordinary sales volumes. The company regularly distributes videotaped interviews with top salespeople who offer tips and advice. Frequent staff meetings are used as workshops for associates to compare, examine, and discuss sales techniques, and to perform skits in which they play the roles of salesperson and customer. For example, the Washington state region's personnel department developed the Sales Training Education Program (STEP) for employees looking for more information from salespeople and department managers. Every month, top sales associates talk about goal setting, marketing, selling, using the phone, and, of course, customer service.

One of the paradoxes at Nordstrom is that while the company insists that all employees are team players who compete on a level playing field, it encourages associates to become star performers. Thus, the flip side of the Nordstrom culture is the intramural (some might say internecine) competition between departments and individuals. From the earliest days, the Nordstroms (all of whom are intensely interested in sports) initiated sales contests to promote rivalry among associates. If the store was overstocked in red pumps, for example, they would have a red pump–selling contest, with the top sales performers rewarded with cash, flowers, dinners, or trips. "In a sense, every day was a contest," Elmer Nordstrom recalled. "Everyone tried to do their best, so that they wouldn't be stuck at the bottom of the list." The company encourages a creative tension among its associates, who have ready access to sales figures from all departments and stores in the Nordstrom chain, so they can compare their performance with that of their colleagues across the selling floor or across the country. Each associate's semi-monthly sales-per-hour figures are posted clearly for all employees to see.

Nordstrom people love to use inter-company competition as a tool for motivating the troops. "We tend to manage by contest," said Jammie Baugh, general manager of Nordstrom's southern California region. "When we have something we want to improve on, then we have a contest." Each division in the company runs monthly "MNS" (Make Nordstrom Special) contests, where good ideas or suggestions are rewarded with cash. The company rewards outstanding sales-per-hour and sales-per-month performances with cash prizes or trips, awards, and good, old-fashioned public praise for a job well done. "You can't ever miss the opportunity to reinforce, recognize, and reward the behavior," said Baugh. Peter Glen, author of the customer service book, *It's Not My Department,* has criticized managers at other companies for forgetting to give recognition to the people they work with. "This is one of the major reasons that service people give bad service to their customers; they reflect the way they are treated by their bosses, and they pass it right on to their customers," wrote Glen.

One example of Nordstrom's "managing by contest" took place in the fourth quarter of 1993, from September 1 to December 24. Nordstrom issued to its employees the "$250,000 Super Service Challenge," which was by far the biggest employee customer service contest in company history. "We wanted to do something fun," said Baugh. Typical of Nordstrom, there were both individual and team cash awards for outstanding customer service in individual categories, such as timeliness of approach to the customer, and team categories, such as store cleanliness. The judges, who posed as customers, included Nordstrom regional general managers (who were assigned stores outside of their region); merchandise managers and top executives (who generally shop at all Nordstrom stores on a regular basis); and employees of an outside professional shopping service.

In order to maintain the momentum and excitement throughout the eighteen-week contest, the company handed out five individual $2,500 cash prizes every two weeks. To be eligible for the drawing, a salesperson had to have received a perfect score from the judges. "You can't imagine the excitement in a store the morning that the prizes were handed out," recalled Baugh. "The store manager would call everybody in the store together and hand out $2,500 to each salesperson who won. It was like Publisher's Clearinghouse." At the end of the contest, a total of $100,000 had been given to forty top salespeople.

The Horton Plaza store in San Diego was judged the store with the best overall shopping experience. As the employees gathered for their regular morning meeting, down the escalator came co-president Ray Johnson with a blown-up check for $100,000, as the Orange Glen High School band played their school fight song. "We do corny stuff," Baugh admitted with a smile and no apologies. A similar scene was duplicated at the Vancouver Mall in Oregon when co-president John Whitacre delivered a $50,000 check for second place. This kind of employee motivation "is the essence of what we're about," said Bruce Nordstrom.

The contest "had a big part to do with the fourth quarter results," said Baugh, when Nordstrom earnings jumped 22.1 percent to $61 million and sales increased 3.6 percent to $1.1 billion. "What we learned, and what became obvious to every single one of us during this contest, was how much opportunity we have. Many of us feel that we still haven't touched the surface of how good we really could be."

■ Goal Setting

Goal setting binds every tier of the inverted pyramid. Sales associates, buyers, and managers perpetually strive to meet personal, departmental, store, and regional goals for the day, month, and year, and to surpass what they did during the same period a year ago. If a department fails to achieve one day's target, the manager raises the following day's target. Peer pressure and personal commitment push the most competitive employees toward higher and higher objectives. Work shifts often start with a reminder of the day's goals; managers regularly quiz sales associates on their individual goals. A store manager (who earns bonuses based on sales increases and expense targets as a percent of sales) might rally the troops by using the public address system to tell a story about someone who just sold $1,000 in cosmetics to one customer.

The *Harvard Business Review* detailed one spirited 1979 sales goal meeting, where the regional manager had asked every department manager and buyer to write down their sales targets for the following year. Although the company is much larger today, the same basic scenario still applies:

> As the figures were called out, the regional manager wrote the amounts against the individual's name on a large chart. Next to the figure in turn was a space on which the regional manager had written his target for each manager. That target figure was kept covered during the initial part of the meeting in which the managers gave their target figures for the year.

Then, amidst great excitement and suspense, the regional manager tore off the slip of paper which covered his target for each individual manager. If the sales target of the manager was under that of the regional manager, the assembly would boo the unfortunate manager. However, if the manager's target was above that of the regional manager, then the group of persons would break out into cheers.

One manager described the scene as being similar to that of a classroom before an exam, or perhaps during an exam, with all the store managers and buyers doing feverish calculations as they heard what their peers were setting as targets and were tempted to revise their own targets.

Top sales associates are just as assiduous today. Shoe salesperson Joe Dover, who described himself as "totally goal-oriented," said those targets keep him "focused." Dover always carries a notebook with him, "so that I know what sales I wrote [recorded] on this day last year. I can trace it back four years to see whether or not I'm growing. Every day, when I walk into the store, I look at the figures I wrote yesterday. Setting a goal only sets the process in motion because goals are constantly changing."

Without goals, said Annette Armony, who sells juniors sportswear in Portland, "you don't have a direction and you lose perspective on why you are there." On the other hand, she cautioned, "if you take a goal too seriously it will ruin the fun of achieving it. Half the challenge of the goal is making it. And when you do make it, you pat yourself on the back. And if you don't make it, you say, 'Next time, I'm going to try a little harder.'"

When Pat McCarthy sets his sales targets every year, his primary objective is to prevent himself from settling for too little. "It is too easy to look for the easy way. As soon as you start looking for shortcuts, you lose the business.

If you work hard and set your mind to it, you can realize those goals. I have never once had a year that I didn't do better than the year before."

As American businesses continue to downsize and each employee has to pull his or her own weight, many companies are following the Nordstrom example. According to a January 30, 1994, article in the *New York Times,* many management consultants are counseling their corporate clients to require employees to either fulfill expectations or find employment elsewhere. "Most companies are moving in the direction that if you don't meet the goals, you're let go," the *Times* quoted Claudia Wyatt, the director of compensation consulting for the Midwest for the Wyatt Company. She added that more and more companies "have been giving employees more responsibilities for setting their own goals."

■ Recognition and Praise

At Nordstrom, the best salespeople achieve the status of Pacesetter. Pacesetters meet or surpass the sales-volume goal for their specific department for the one-year period from December 16 through December 15 of the following year. (For example, the 1994 average Pacesetter target in the women's apparel division was $385,000.) To maintain Pacesetter status, each year Nordstrom raises the target-goal figures, depending on how many people achieved Pacesetter the year before. Generally, 8 to 12 percent of the salespeople in each division make Pacesetter. Kazumi Ohara, who manages the Chanel handbags department in the downtown Seattle store, has been a Pacesetter for many years. To track her goal of reaching the Pacesetter target, Ohara divides the pay year by quarters, subdivides the quarters by six two-week pay periods, and then records her earnings for each pay period in her personal book. She boosts her target level every year. Pacesetters are given a certificate of merit, an event or an outing in their honor, business cards emblazoned with the Pacesetter designation, and a 33 percent discount credit card (13 percent more than the regular employee discount) for one year. First-year Pacesetters also get a special leather case binder for their personal customer book (which will be explained later in greater detail) and a lapel pin. People who have achieved Pacesetter for five years, ten years, and so on, receive more generous awards.

The company rewards other top performers with incentives such as cash and gifts. Every month, each store manager selects Customer Service All-Stars based on individuals' sales volumes and the level of support they give their co-workers. All-Stars are given a 33 percent store discount for one year. Based on three criteria—sales volume, customer service, and teamwork, Nordstrom rewards people with the best work shift schedule. The definition of the "best" shift depends on the individual. Some prefer the busiest times; others opt for shifts that best fit into their life. (The competition for shifts among salespeople became one of the issues Nordstrom had to deal with when the company found itself in a battle in 1989 and 1990 with the union representing its six Seattle-area stores. This episode will be discussed in detail in Chapter 6.)

When individuals and departments have a successful day or are "on target" in reaching their goals, they are praised over the store intercom during the morning announcements before the store opens. Monthly store pow-wows serve as a kind of revival meeting, where customers' letters of appreciation are read and positive achievements are recognized, while co-workers whoop and cheer for each other. On the other hand, letters of complaint about

Nordstrom's customer service are also read over the intercom (omitting the names of the offending salespeople). "That's how we learn that the customer is our boss," said McCarthy. "Nordstrom's name is on my paycheck, but I'm paid by the customer."

■ Heroics

Essential to passing on the Nordstrom corporate culture and mythology are "heroics"—true tales of incredible customer service, such as warming up a customer's car in the dead of winter. Employees who witness a colleague giving customer service above and beyond the call of duty are encouraged to write up a description of what they saw and submit it to their managers. Frequent recipients of heroics are elected to the weekly V.I.P. Club or selected "Employee of the Month," with their pictures mounted in the customer service office in the store where they work. The week's collection of heroics are printed up and circulated among associates. The purpose of heroics is to give Nordstrom people a standard to aspire to—and even surpass. "If you see a great example, you're going to imitate that," said Len Kuntz.

Here's one notable, but not atypical, example of a heroic: A customer, who was about to catch a flight at Seattle-Tacoma Airport, inadvertently left her airline ticket at the counter in one of Nordstrom's women's apparel departments. Discovering the ticket, her Nordstrom sales associate immediately phoned the airline and asked the service representative if she could track down the customer at the airport and write her another ticket. No, she could not. So the Nordstrom salesperson jumped into a cab, rode out to the airport (at her own expense), located the customer, and delivered the ticket herself. (Nordstrom later reimbursed her for the cab fare.)

■ Loyalty and Ownership

The Nordstrom family has always considered employee loyalty something to be earned, not expected. Because the brothers felt that the commitment to loyalty started with them, they wanted to provide an opportunity for their employees to make more money than any other retail salespeople. When shopping the New York shoe markets, Everett encouraged young buyers to develop their own ideas and make their own decisions. Elmer used to tell the story of what happened when one shoe manufacturer's sales staff showed their line to both Everett and a young buyer of women's shoes (the store's biggest department), and then turned to Everett for his reaction. "Don't talk to me," said Everett, "this is my buyer." The sales representatives then turned their eyes toward the nervous twenty-two-year-old buyer. "After that, the fellow worked his heart out for the company," Elmer recalled.

Nordstrom's employee profit-sharing retirement plan inspires motivation and encourages loyalty. "We'd like to make it easy to retire for people who have done a great job for us," said Bruce Nordstrom. The program began in 1952 when the brothers wanted to make sure that employees would have money for retirement beyond Social Security, and to help the company attract better personnel. (The Nordstrom plan was copied from one that had been used for years by Sears Roebuck, but while Sears required employee contributions, Nordstrom did not.) "It was a natural development that reflected our basic philosophy: the better we treated our people, the better our people performed," recalled Elmer Nordstrom. In the beginning, profit-sharing funds weren't made available until the employee turned sixty-five, but today, 20 percent of an employee's profit-sharing account is vested after three years; 40 percent after four years; 60 percent after five years; 80

percent after six years; and 100 percent after seven years. Based on the previous year's earnings, Nordstrom's board of directors decides how much the contribution will be. In 1994, the company contributed almost 22 percent of its earnings—or $44.0 million—to the profit-sharing trust. (When the company experiences a subpar year, Nordstrom family members take substantial pay cuts, but still fund the profit-sharing program.) Like everything else at Nordstrom, the profit-sharing plan has built-in financial incentives that encourage industriousness, teamwork, customer service, and expense savings. Because contributions are made to the plan directly from the company's net earnings, employees have an incentive to be productive and cost-conscious. (Remember, Nordstrom's shrinkage rate is only a shade under 1.5 percent of sales.) That also promotes loyalty because employees share ownership. Today, some longtime employees retire with profit-sharing totals in the high six figures. All employees who work more than a thousand hours per year, participate in the plan.

The other part of the Profit Sharing Retirement Plan is called P.S. Plus, a 401(k) plan that enables employees to contribute from 1 percent to 10 percent of their annual compensation to a tax-deferred investment retirement account, which includes contributions made by the company. The amount paid is determined by the board of directors and the individual employee's length of service and income during the year. Nordstrom matches twenty-five cents on the dollar on the first 6 percent of pay that an employee defers. In 1994, those matching funds reached $4.825 million. (That number is subtracted from the 22 percent of earnings designated for the profit-sharing trust.)

Today, with employment in most industries in such a state of flux, the only way people will be loyal to a company is if they are given appreciation, respect, good pay, and a piece of the action. "When you have ownership, people give a damn," said co-president John Whitacre. Bob Middlemas, manager of the Midwest region, noted that "as time goes on, and the balances in the employees' profit-sharing accounts grow, so does their concern with how the company is doing, because there is a lot at stake for them personally. When they see somebody waste a supply, like throwing a perfectly good bag in the garbage, there is more of an awareness of protecting the company's assets."

In an article in the *New York Times*, Henry R. Kravis and George R. Roberts, founding partners of the investment banking firm Kohlberg, Kravis, Roberts, & Company, wrote, ". . . ownership is the most powerful incentive for business change. Corporations achieve better performance over the long term when employees share the risks and rewards of ownership. This is accountability *from the inside out* [their italics], and it works. Ownership focuses attention on the good of the organization like nothing else can."

KEYS TO SUCCESS

The Nordstrom culture sets employees free. The company believes that people will work hard when they are given the freedom to do their job the way they think it should be done, and when they can treat customers they way *they* like to be treated. Nordstrom believes that too many rules, regulations, paperwork, and strict channels of communication erode employee incentive. Without those shackles, Nordstrom people can operate like entrepreneurial shopkeepers.

- Nordstrom is informally organized as an "inverted pyramid," with the top positions occupied by the customers and the salespeople, and the bottom position filled by the co-chairmen. Every tier of the pyramid supports the sales staff.
- Empowering the people on the sales floor with the freedom to accept returned merchandise is the most obvious illustration of the Nordstrom culture because it directly impacts the public.
- The unconditional money-back guarantee is designed for the 98 percent of customers who are honest.
- Nordstrom tears down barriers. Salespeople are free to sell merchandise to their customers in any department throughout the store. This promotes continuity in the relationship between the salesperson and the customer.
- Like everyone at Nordstrom, department managers begin their career as salespeople to learn what's required to take care of the customer. This sends the signal that management values the role of salesperson.
- Managers are encouraged to have a feeling of ownership about their department. They are responsible for hiring, training, coaching, nurturing, and evaluating their sales team, and are expected to spend some of

their time on the selling floor, interacting with the customers and the sales staff.

- Buying at Nordstrom is decentralized, which means that buyers in each region are given the freedom to acquire merchandise that reflects local lifestyles and tastes. Because buyers are responsible for just a few stores, they can afford to take a chance on a unique item without fear of jeopardizing the bottom line.

- Empowerment for getting the right merchandise in the store begins not in the buying office, but on the floor—at the point of the sale. Nordstrom encourages entrepreneurial salespeople to provide input to their manager and buyer on fashion direction, styles, quantities, sizes, and colors.

- Employee compensation is based on sales commissions. The Nordstrom brothers felt that the best way to attract and retain self-starters was by paying them according to their ability.

- An employee profit-sharing retirement plan inspires motivation, and encourages loyalty. Because contributions are made to the plan *directly* from the company's net earnings, employees have an incentive to be productive and cost conscious.

- Goal-setting is essential to the culture. Employees at every level are perpetually striving to meet or surpass personal, departmental, store, and regional goals for the day, month, and year. Peer pressure and personal commitment push competitive employees toward constantly higher goals.

- Employees have access to sales figures from all departments and stores in the chain, so they can compare their performances.

- Outstanding sales performances are rewarded with prizes and praise, as are good ideas and suggestions.

- Top salespeople are encouraged to help others with sales techniques, and building a customer base.

What's Inside

Creating an Inviting Place

Walking to the Nordstrom store in the Garden State Plaza in Paramus, New Jersey, a woman shopper stops at the espresso bar just outside the store for a latte coffee drink. After finishing her latte, she enters the store as the glass doors open automatically for her. She walks over to the intimate apparel department, pausing for a moment to run her hand across the silk lingerie. She heads over to the concierge's desk, where a gentleman standing ahead of her is inquiring about hotels in the vicinity. After he leaves, the concierge checks the coat of our woman shopper, who then requests the paging of a friend, and makes a reservation for lunch at The Garden Court restaurant, which is located on the store's third floor. As she strolls toward the escalator, she lingers with a group of resting shoppers, who are perched on upholstered leather sofas and chairs in a waiting area, listening to a tuxedoed man at the grand piano play "As Time Goes By."

Ascending the escalator, the shopper scans each floor, taking a mental inventory of the clearly marked departments that encircle the escalator well, which is dramatically designed with marble detailing and mahogany

131

columns and accents. She gets off the escalator on the second floor and heads toward the cosmetics department, where she pauses long enough to sample a spritz of the new Donna Karan perfume. Her next stop is at Spa Nordstrom, to make an appointment for a facial, manicure, and massage. By the time she buys a pair of shoes and a matching dress, eats lunch, and indulges herself at the spa, she's spent several hours at the mall and has never set foot outside of Nordstrom. And that's just the way Nordstrom wants it, because we have just described the ideal Nordstrom shopping experience, where men and women are invited not only to buy the merchandise, but also to relax and linger, their Nordstrom credit card at the ready.

This scenario did not happen by accident. What's inside the store—the layout, design, display fixtures, amenities, and, of course, the merchandise—is yet another facet of customer service the Nordstrom way. Nordstrom likes to create "a memorable experience" at their stores, a lesson that should be heeded by virtually any business that deals with the public.

As simple as this concept sounds, some corners of the retail industry are just catching on to it. In a May 1993 *Women's Wear Daily* article, Dennis Toffolo, president of Detroit-based Hudson's department store, said that his company's market research showed that customers want more seating, better lighting, larger fitting rooms, clear, wide aisles, and "a residential feeling." Even mass merchants like Kmart and Caldor have begun to add those conveniences to their stores, thanks to the results of extensive market research and consumer polling. They all could have saved themselves a lot of expense by foregoing their voluminous studies and instead visiting virtually any Nordstrom store, because Nordstrom has provided customers with those amenities since the late 1970s. In fact, some of the best ideas for making the shopping experience more enjoyable—such as a concierge desk to assist customers—were generated not by interior designers but by Nordstrom salespeople, who know full well that they are the ultimate beneficiary of customer comfort.

Nordstrom has some of the most modern stores in the country because its most dramatic expansion came in the late 1970s and 1980s, when financing was readily available to build new stores in new malls and very few competitors were matching Nordstrom's spending. From 1978 through 1995, Nordstrom opened forty-six full-line stores in California, the Washington, D.C. area, New Jersey, New York, suburban Chicago, suburban Minneapolis, and Indianapolis. As the company expanded, so did the size of its stores. In the early 1970s, the average Nordstrom store area was 60,000 to 70,000 square feet; today it's about 200,000 square feet.

Store construction at Nordstrom reached the peak of elegance in the late 1980s, when affluence was in full bloom, with the construction of the luxurious downtown San Francisco Centre store at 5th and Market Streets. Built for an estimated $73 million, the 336,000-square-foot store—by far Nordstrom's largest—was the first major U.S. department store that started several levels above the ground floor of a building. The store mixed classic European and contemporary influences, such as Italian marble and granite in ivory, gray, and black; custom carpets with Florentine borders; statues in the elevator lobbies; traditional wood furnishings; and modern fabrics. A local artist was commissioned to paint a round ceiling fresco for the couture department. The two-floor, clubby men's apparel department featured dark, polished wood floors and paneling, English furnishings, an authentic English-style pub, and a working fireplace—one of the few in all of retailing. (There's also one in the Polo/Ralph Lauren store on Madison Avenue in Manhattan.)

From the beginning of its major expansion phase, Nordstrom designed its stores with a "layman's eye," rather than relying on traditional department store aesthetics or extensive research, explained Barden Erickson, a retired Nordstrom vice-president for store design and a founder of The Callison Partnership, a Seattle-based firm that has designed more than sixty Nordstrom stores. "We did almost everything by feel, by trial and error." During its aggressive expansion period, Nordstrom's stores were constantly being remodeled and fine-tuned, and if any design aspect was found to be flawed, "two weeks after that store opened we would be changing it," said Erickson. "Plus, when we put in something [in one store] that was really good, merchandise managers would want to get that in their stores. Because of our growth, we had the ability to do that." During that period of rapid growth, the Nordstroms themselves, particularly John Nordstrom, strongly influenced the philosophy, aesthetic design proposals, and construction details of every department in every store. Each significant detail was subject to their review and approval.

Unlike the mythical customer who opened this chapter, fewer people these days are shopping for the fun of it, and those who are shopping have indicated that they don't want to sort through hundreds of thousands of square feet of retail space to find what they're looking for. In the 1970s, "shopping was entertainment," said Laura Petrucci, of the Marketing Corporation of America. "In the 1980s, it was the quest for trendy merchandise. In the 1990s, it's a mission: find it, buy it, and get out." And as Professor Theodore D. Kemper wrote in the *New York Times*, "We foolishly . . . treat the consumer's time as a cost-free good in the same careless way that we used to treat our precious air and water. . . . This omission is costly."

Consequently, Nordstrom continues to tinker with store design in order to reflect changing times and consumer tastes, with an emphasis on saving time so that the customer can get in and out of the store as quickly and easily as possible. The 160,000-square-foot store in the Annapolis Mall, which opened in 1994, is two floors instead of the usual three. "When we design a store," said John Nordstrom, who is considered something of a student of store design and customer reaction, "a lot of our vendors don't necessarily want to go to the third floor, they all want to be on the first floor, and if they can't be on the first floor, they want to be on the second floor." He does not "necessarily think we have to make our stores as big as we're making them. I've been one for making them a little bit smaller and a little bit more efficient, trying to use all that square footage rather than just making them bigger and bigger and bigger."

In another effort to become more customer-friendly, Nordstrom has been experimenting with opening up the space in the display areas in some of its cosmetics departments. The traditional glass counters are being replaced with "I"-shaped islands that have a makeup station on each end. Down through the middle of the islands are products on shelves, information signs, and clearly marked prices. The inspiration for this "open-sell" concept came out of a customer focus group, where some participants said they did not shop in a cosmetics department because they found the experience too intimidating.

"They felt that they had to be committed to buy when they walked up to the counter," said Dale C. Crichton, Nordstrom's vice-president in charge of cosmetics. "They just couldn't browse in cosmetics very well and couldn't really see the price points; they had to ask for it. We opened up the department so that the customer could browse if she wanted to or be assisted if she wanted to. She can very easily touch the merchandise. There are testers so she can try the product. In this day and age, the customer is busy and is sometimes looking for a quick transaction. But if she has more time, then we are there for her, too. We haven't reduced our sales staff at all because we still want to provide great service." In the cosmetics department of its newer stores, Nordstrom has built a special "Cosmetics Activities Room" where customers can visit with in-store beauty directors for private consultations.

■ What's Outside/What's Inside

Nordstrom has always emphasized the importance of exterior store architecture, rather than presenting a plain box. While many of their department store mall neighbors eschew display windows that face the mall parking lot, Nordstrom emphasizes those windows, because they contribute to a feeling of openness and brightness that carries throughout the store. To continue that theme, the company often builds windows that open onto the customer service area and the tailor alteration shops.

Nordstrom stores are not cookie-cutter buildings. In order to better fit into their new neighborhoods, store facades, whenever possible, complement the area of the country where they are located—from the southern California mission-style of the Santa Barbara store to the arched entryway, double cornice, and mansard roof of the Pentagon City store near Washington, D.C., which takes its design inspiration from the famous five-sided home of the United States Department of Defense, located across the street from the mall. Store interiors often show off the works of local artists.

Nordstrom store ambiance is not elitist because the company has always wanted to appeal to as many customers as possible. This desire stems from the family's roots in Seattle, a city that prides itself on its determinedly egalitarian, middle-class sensibility. Bruce Nordstrom liked to point out that even when his mother, Elizabeth, reached her eighties, she preferred shopping in departments that attracted young people because "she didn't want to shop where old people did," said Bruce. "She liked shopping next to somebody who knew what was going on in clothing. If we were an old-fashioned store that just sold the things she wanted, she wouldn't like the atmosphere."

Nordstrom sells "nice clothes for nice people," Morley Safer said in his *60 Minutes* feature on the company. Apparel, shoes, and accessories are merchandised in a variety of departments, depending upon the customer's age, fashion taste, personal style, and price range. There is plenty of affordable merchandise (sixty dollars and under) for young women and young men. Departments are arranged according to lifestyle. For example, the Savvy department represents young, fun, fast, fashion. The Collectors department, on the other hand, appeals to the designer customer, with offerings from the likes of Donna Karan, Calvin Klein, Claude Montana, Gianni Versace, and Thiery Mugler. The "Collectors" name implies that the woman who purchases designer clothing is a connoisseur—a collector—of beautiful and fine things, and is likely to be interested in art and cultural trends. Men's wear also runs the gamut, from moderately priced sportswear to Polo and Oxxford wool suits. Footwear ranges from inexpensive boat shoes to luxurious Italian slingback pumps. Because the company knows that price is still an issue with many customers, signs are strategically posted at store entrances to reassure shoppers that "Nordstrom will not be undersold" and will match the competition's price on the same item.

■ Comfort and Ease

Even before customers enter the store, Nordstrom has been thinking about making things smooth for them, beginning with adequate parking within easy walking distance. "We try to protect our sphere of influence around our store to make sure our customers are well served by the parking," said David P. Lindsey, vice-president of store planning and a former partner in The Callison Partnership architectural firm. During busy sales times, Nordstrom offers valet parking for its customers.

Convenience and openness are trademarks of Nordstrom store design. "When customers first come into the store, we've got about fifteen seconds to get them excited about it," said John Nordstrom. "First, are they able to meander through the store without impediments, such as narrow aisles? When they're walking down an aisle, and another customer is coming the other way, do they have enough room to pass? If the answer is no, all of a sudden they're distracted. Instead of looking at the nice sweater, they've got a stroller banging them in the ankles. When they think about our store, they don't think of jostling and banging, they think of it as a pleasant experience. What's that worth?"

Consequently, Nordstrom wants to make it as easy as possible for customers to circulate and shop through the entire store, and for sales associates to help them do just that. Departments are designed, and merchandise better organized, edited, and more clearly defined by lifestyle so that the presentation is instantly understood and a wardrobe can be more quickly assembled by the entrepreneurial salespeople who implement customer service the Nordstrom way.

Store layouts typically resemble a wheel. The hub is the escalator well and the spokes are the marbled aisles that lead directly back to each of the thirty or so departments. The subtleties and details make the shopping experience easy and convenient. Aisles provide ample room for customers to browse (and for people in wheelchairs or parents with strollers to get around) and give shoppers the freedom to circle the store and to plunge into the center of each individual department. (Nordstrom believes that if you can lure customers to the perimeter walls at the back of the store, they are more apt to make a purchase.) By making the aisles around the escalator wide enough, "if someone wants to walk all the way around the store, they're not fighting through traffic, even on the busiest day. That's important because, sometimes, that's the only time we get that customer in the store," said John Nordstrom.

To make it easier to get around for people with strollers or wheelchairs, the waiting areas around elevators are extra wide and the elevators themselves are larger than average. Nordstrom stores usually have two elevators, which give customers faster service; the second elevator serves as a back-up if one is out of order. Escalators are forty-two inches wide—compared to the thirty-six inches of most other department stores—which are roomy enough for spouses or children to ride next to each other. Unobstructed sight lines enable the customers riding on the escalators to quickly scrutinize the whole selling floor. Large graphics on curtain walls clearly show the names of departments. To make locating departments even easier, Nordstrom introduced an interactive, computerized store directory and map that enables a customer to locate whatever department she needs and tell her how to get there from where she is. The first of these directories, which was developed by Nordstrom, was introduced in 1994 in the Mall of America store in Bloomington, Minnesota. In the newer stores, such as in Old Orchard Center (Skokie, Illinois), cashier stations come with pull-out shelves that make it easier for customers in wheelchairs to make purchase transactions.

Unlike large retailers who close off their departments with walls or dividers, most of Nordstrom's departments are free-standing. They are defined by lighted curtain walls, secondary aisles, upholstered lounge seating, custom-designed hardwood, bronze, and plate glass showcases; antique furnishings and display fixtures are built low, so as not to obscure shoppers' view of other departments or sales associates' views of customers. Spaces in virtually every department are made warm and homey by the furnishings, as well as plants, plush carpeting, wainscoting, and poster art that Nordstrom has commissioned specifically for the store. Apparel and footwear are presented in succinct, understated visual displays that change regularly to maintain interest among frequent shoppers. Throughout the store, the merchandise is enhanced by track lighting. Although other retailers are now catching on to the aesthetic qualities of track lighting, few use it as innovatively and extensively as Nordstrom.

Secondary aisles that run through the back of the departments are about ten feet from the back wall. "We've spent all this money on the store; let's make every square foot as important as we can, rather than just the front end of the store," said John Nordstrom. "In the old days, we used to push everything toward the front; the back of the store was only sale stuff. That's nuts. We can be more efficient than that. A lot of times we can get more merchandise on the floor, because we're using the back third of the department." Today, along the back walls, the merchandise is highlighted and romanced, like artwork in a gallery, by ambient lighting and woven cotton, wool, or silk fabric coverings in warm, natural tones.

At the end of extended aisles, Nordstrom prefers to situate destination areas such as a gift department, restaurant, dressing room, or lounge, rather than run the aisle into a wall. "When there's nothing down the other end, it's jarring to the customer," said John Nordstrom. "But if there's something down there, they want to see what it is."

Comfort and ease are the guiding principles behind the design of Nordstrom's large, carpeted dressing rooms, fitting rooms, and customer lounges, which are furnished with upholstered chairs and/or sofas. Fitting rooms in the stores' more fashionable ready-to-wear departments include tables, table lamps, and telephones. "Telephones have become a part of customer service," said sales associate Van Mensah. "I have many customers who need to make international calls and I'm able to put them through."

Particular attention is given to the lighting of the mirrors in the dressing rooms. Nordstrom uses a combination of incandescent and fluorescent lights so that the customer can see the actual colors of the item she is purchasing. By minimizing the use of incandescent lighting and controlling the coolness of the dressing rooms with a dedicated thermostat—separate from the thermostats controlling the sales floor and the adjoining rooms—customers don't get hot and sweaty while trying on clothes. Although independent thermostats add to Nordstrom's costs, they also add to the customer's comfort. And she is more likely to continue to try on clothes, if she is comfortable. "The whole point of everything we do is to make the customer happy for the long haul. If people are satisfied and excited about the experience of shopping at Nordstrom, they will come back. And if you haven't created that atmosphere, they won't come back. It's just that simple," said David Lindsey, vice president of store planning.

Because parents with children also require more room, the dressing rooms and lounges (both men's and women's) are large enough to accommodate strollers and diaper-changing tables. All stores have special rooms for nursing mothers and newer stores incorporate "family" bathrooms where a parent can accompany his or her child of the opposite sex. Some Nordstrom stores equip their children's areas with toys, coloring tables, television sets, video games, and built-in helium containers for blowing up balloons; in other units, kids can design and sign their own floor tiles, which are then installed in the floor of the department.

Nordstrom's spacious design comes with a sacrifice of square footage devoted exclusively to selling. By comparison, Macy's claims that about 70 percent of its total store square footage is used for selling, compared to a little more than 50 percent at Nordstrom, although newer Nordstrom stores do about 7 percent more, thanks to more efficient design. On the other hand, Nordstrom packs its selling spaces with the highest value of inventory per-square-foot of any specialty apparel retailer in the country—20 to 30 percent more than the competition—as well as more salespeople and cash registers.

"The percentage of the floor covered with merchandise is deceiving," said John Nordstrom. "I think that Macy's and [other department stores] don't measure their stores like we do. I think that if we measured one of their stores, we would find that it's less efficient than our stores." Again, he believed that the most important thing is for customers to be able to maneuver through the store and look at the merchandise. "Some of our buyers and merchandisers say they don't have enough space in their department and ask to have the aisle taken out. We're not taking away any space by putting the aisle in, because we've got to get the customers through there, anyway. All we're doing is organizing the space to give [buyers and merchandisers] more frontage for merchandise on both sides of that aisle. When I finally get them convinced and we put it in, they just love it, because of all the additional traffic coming through their department."

With its heritage as a shoe company, Nordstrom's footwear departments (most stores have four or five separate departments) are its showplaces; women's shoes are always located near the most prominent store entrance to the mall. Because shoes are the most important customer draw (after all, most people have a hard time finding a pair that fits), the company devotes about three times more space to its women's shoe department than its competitors and fills it up with more inventory than any other. The Mall of America store in Minneapolis stocks over 250,000 different sizes, styles, and colors; downtown Seattle carries over 300,000 pairs. The greater the selection, the less chance that a customer will leave the store disappointed. "You can stock a pump in navy blue and black calf," said John Nordstrom, "but if the customer wants it in black patent leather, and you don't have it in black patent leather, you don't make the sale. And you have to have it in her size. The last thing a sales associate wants to do is to walk back out to the sales floor and tell the customer that you don't have the shoe she wants." At newer Nordstrom stores, half the footwear inventory in a department is stocked directly behind the departments, making it easier and less time-consuming—for both the sales associate and the customer; the other half is stocked in rooms located on mezzanines off the sales floor. Since so much of the stockroom merchandise is nearby, sales associates don't have to hustle up and down stairs all day. "We can get in and out of the shoe stockroom in a couple of minutes, if that," said Deborah Kirsch of the Oakbrook Mall store. "Although we have many, many shoes in the stockroom, we have lots of people back there to help us locate the right one."

Because Nordstrom carries so many shoes, and because most feet are so tough to fit, Nordstrom knows that customers are going to be in the footwear department for a while, so they make sure the customers are comfortable. Seating is sturdy enough to withstand the constant wear that's a fact of life in a bustling shoe department. While most other retailers fill their shoe departments with a line of half a dozen or so straightback chairs, Nordstrom creates a homey parlor or lounge feeling with plushly upholstered sofas and as many as thirty-five upholstered chairs. These chairs are custom-made because the typical department store chair is not cushy, durable, or high enough to meet Nordstrom specifications. Chair legs and arms are made a bit taller than average and the seating is firmer, which makes it easier for a person to stand up. Consequently, customers need only focus on how the shoe feels; not whether they'll have difficulty getting up out of the chair.

"Customers will comment on how comfortable the seating is," said Deborah Kirsch. "A lot of times husbands and boyfriends will sit there waiting in the department or over by the piano. Or get their shoes shined for only $1.25. That kind of layout gives you comfort. People will stay a little longer and try on more shoes if they are comfortable. I've had the experience at another company, where they had the standard chairs, and the husband or boyfriend would get impatient and say, 'C'mon, c'mon, we've got to get out of here.'"

Another way Nordstrom keeps people in the store, enhances the shopping environment, and generates profits is by offering a variety of food and restaurant services, which are a direct response to changing consumer needs. "The traditional department store was built for the consumer market of women who left home [to shop] and then went back home after two or three hours," said Mimi Lieber, a consultant with LAR Management Consultants, in a *Women's Wear Daily* article. "That's very different from how we live today, where we are away from home for long periods of time. More people are shopping with children and more are doing lunch-hour shopping, which means they also have to get something to eat." Barden Erickson, the former vice-president of store design, agreed: "When customers are spending the amount of time they do in our stores, you need a place for them to sit down and relax, have a meal, have some coffee." (Nordstrom charges only twenty-five cents for a regular cup of coffee because Jim Nordstrom doesn't like restaurants "that charge a dollar for a cup of coffee when it costs only a few cents.") Mass merchandisers, in particular, are catching on to the benefits of in-store restaurants. Wal-Mart Stores has teamed up with McDonald's Corporation; Kmart with Little Caesar's Pizza; Jamesway with Burger King; and Caldor's with Nathan's Famous Hot Dogs.

Nordstrom has been in the food business since 1979, when the company took over management of the cafes in its stores from an outside company. Today, Nordstrom is one of the Pacific Northwest's largest caterers, with a 26,000-square-foot office and kitchen complex that includes three kitchens and a floral design facility. The company currently has four restaurant concepts, with about half of the stores offering at least two of them. The Espresso Bar, which is generally located at an entrance outside the store, purveys gourmet coffees, Italian sodas, and pastries to Nordstrom customers as well as people walking through the mall. Cafe Nordstrom serves soups, salads, sandwiches, pastries, and beverages in a cafeteria format. The Garden Court offers full-service dining, with fresh, seasonal produce and seafood in an elegant atmosphere. The Pub is a clubby dining area that serves coffee and breakfast items from 9:30 to 11:30 A.M.; and sandwiches, salads, cocktails, stouts, and ales the rest of the day, accompanied by television monitors showing live coverage of sporting events. If customers have to wait for a table, Nordstrom prefers they continue shopping throughout the store. So, once customers make their reservation, Nordstrom gives them a beeper to alert them when their table is ready.

Nordstrom's consideration for customer comfort was summed up by a Seattle writer named J. Glenn Evans, who penned this poem, entitled "A Place to Rest":*

> I followed my wife
> while she shopped
> From store to store
> from window to window
> she went
>
> I the great man
> was spent
> The flesh pulled on my bones
> like two bags of cement
>
> At last I found a chair
> Heaven only
> could have been more fair
>
> Of all the stores
> Nordstrom was best
> They gave a husband
> a place to rest

*Used with permission of the author.

"All of these images, collectively, convey the persona of our store and what we are trying to be," said David Lindsey, the current vice-president of store design. "We believe in portraying an inviting image of timelessness, comfort, and warmth. Because we are designing for a much longer [time] curve, our stores have an updated traditional look, just like our clothing. When you put on an updated traditional suit, it should be immediately comfortable; you should look good and feel good—today and tomorrow. You have a favorite suit or tie. We want to be your favorite store."

KEYS TO SUCCESS

What's inside the store—the layout, design, display fixtures, amenities, and merchandise—is another facet of customer service the Nordstrom way. Nordstrom likes to create "a memorable experience" at their stores. This is a lesson that can and should be heeded by virtually any business that deals with the public. Store design and merchandising take many forms:

- Convenience and openness. When customers enter the store, Nordstrom has about 15 seconds to get them excited. Consequently, Nordstrom wants to make it as easy as possible for customers to circulate and shop throughout the entire store—and for sales associates to help them. Departments are defined, designed, and merchandised by lifestyle so that the presentation is instantly understood and a wardrobe can be quickly assembled.

- Display windows that face the mall parking lot contribute to a feeling of openness and brightness that is carried throughout the store. To continue that theme, the company often builds windows that open onto the customer service area and the tailor alteration shops.

- Nordstrom stores feature more seating, better lighting, larger fitting rooms, wider aisles, and a more residential feeling.

- For customer comfort, seating in the footwear department is sturdily built to withstand constant wear. A homey lounge feeling is created with custom-made upholstered sofas and chairs. Because the legs and arms of Nordstrom's chairs are taller than average and the seating is firmer, customers don't have to worry whether they'll have difficulty getting up out of the chair. They are free to focus on how the shoe fits.

6

A Company of Entrepreneurs

The "Nordies" Versus the "Clock-Punchers"

For many years, Betsy Sanders was vice-president and general manager for Nordstrom's southern California division. As a retail industry leader, she frequently met with her competitors for United Way meetings and the like, and on those occasions she would invariably be taken aside by one of her competitors, who wanted to know, confidentially, where Nordstrom found all those gung-ho sales people. "We got our people from the same employee pool they did," recalled Sanders, now a retail consultant and a member of the board of directors of Wal-Mart Stores. "The difference between Nordstrom and its competitors was that the Nordstroms didn't go around talking about how wretched their people were. The Nordstroms thought they had great people. And look at the result."

Someone once asked Martha Wikstrom, general manager of Nordstrom's Capital region, whether she thought Nordstrom employees were exceptional people or whether they worked in an atmosphere where they were expected to be exceptional, and therefore performed on that level.

"I think we have some exceptional people and I think we have some average people who work at an exceptional level and, given another set of circumstances, wouldn't be able to do that," said Wikstrom. "Our culture supports that."

David Butler, a shoe salesperson in the Tacoma store, described Nordstrom sales associates as, "ordinary people who have decided to set extraordinary goals. It's up to the individual. You can give people all the tools in the world, but only some people will take command." Butler has seen many new employees who didn't appear to be able to sell a pair of shoes become Pacesetters in their first year at Nordstrom. On the other hand, "there are guys who have worked here for many years who don't believe they can make Pacesetter. The most successful people may not have all the qualifications, but they have the enthusiasm and energy and like coming to work."

■ Who Are These People?

Previous retail experience or a college degree has never been a prerequisite for succeeding at Nordstrom. In the 1920s and 1930s, the Nordstrom brothers recruited "fiery producers, tough guys, men who had to work hard to put bread on the table," Elmer Nordstrom recalled. Hiring these self-described "shoe dogs," who were attracted by Nordstrom's commission sales, "was usually a shot in the dark. In most cases, we just looked them over, gave them a shoe horn, and watched how they performed."

Where do today's "Nordies" (as many of them like be to called) come from? Some were lured away from the competition. At the time Nordstrom announced the opening of its first store in the New York metropolitan area, Art Langelotti was working for a specialty men's retail store that was part of the Hartmarx Corporation retail chain. Hartmarx paid for Langelotti and his colleagues to travel to the Tysons Corner Mall to get a first-hand look at Nordstrom. Attracted by Nordstrom's commission structure, which provided "more incentive to sell harder and do more work," Langelotti joined the company as a men's clothing sales associate in the Garden State Mall in Paramus, New Jersey, and doubled his income in his first year.

Deborah Kirsch, who works in Brass Plum Shoes, at the Oak Brook Mall in Chicago, tells a similar story. Her one-time employer—a Chicago area retail footwear chain—prepared its sales staff for Nordstrom's 1992 debut in the Midwest with a series of meetings that dissected the Nordstrom operation. Kirsch was so impressed that she was among Nordstrom's first new hires—along with several of her colleagues. Today, she is a Pacesetter.

Other Nordies are home-grown. Typical is Patrice Nagasawa of the Savvy department in the suburban Seattle Bellevue Square Mall. Nagasawa worked part-time at Nordstrom through her four years at the University of Washington (where she earned a business degree) and found that, "working at Nordstrom could be a career, because I enjoyed it and was good at it." She is a Pacesetter All-Star, which means that she's the corporate sales leader for her department, which stocks fashion-forward designer apparel.

David Butler, a modern-day, self-described "shoe dog," started with Nordstrom just out of high school in 1968 when the department manager "gave me a shoe horn and said, 'Let's see what you can do.'" Today, Butler sells almost $900,000 worth of shoes a year.

Kazumi Ohara, manager of the Chanel boutique in the downtown Seattle store, used to work for an insurance company.

McCarthy, as we previously pointed out, worked for several years as a youth corrections counsellor.

The qualities that Nordstrom is looking for in its employees couldn't be more basic.

First of all, the company wants its associates to be *nice.* "We can hire nice people and teach them to sell," Bruce Nordstrom likes to say, "but we can't hire salespeople and teach them to be nice." The corollary to that Nordstromism is "hire the smile and train the skill." The company is somewhat reluctant to take on men and women with sales experience because they might have a hard time adjusting to the Nordstrom culture. "We didn't use to feel that way," Jim Nordstrom said. "But as time went on, we learned that people who haven't worked for anybody else haven't learned to say 'no' to the customer."

Because the company assumes that people are best trained by their parents, it provides little in the way of a formalized training program. The result is that workers are sorted out by a natural selection process where only the fittest survive. "You are thrown out there and either you catch it or you don't," said Joyce Johnson from the Corte Madera store in Marin County.

Potential Nordies, said co-president John Whitacre, "have to prove to us and to themselves that they really believe in helping others and genuinely like to give customer service." Typical is Annette Armory, a Pacesetter in the Brass Plum department in Portland's Washington Square store, who considers her job "the easiest in the world because I do what the customer wants."

Nordstrom's best sales associates, who are expected to generate their own traffic, are entrepreneurial self-starters like Kazumi Ohara, who said, "Working at Nordstrom means caring about your business every minute, every hour, and being excited about what you do. Consistency is very important. Carelessness and laziness are a disease. I feel that I have my own little Chanel store, and I will be there no matter what happens. That's the consistency." Selling Chanel handbags, clothing, shoes, and jewelry is fun "because I believe in it," said Ohara, an eight-year Pacesetter, who has recorded as much as $20,000 in sales in one day.

Nordstrom encourages its people "to use their own style, talents, and personality," said Marty Wikstrom. "People are going to care a heckuva lot more about something they have ownership of. They are going to take care of it. It's like renting versus buying. If you own your home, you are going to plant flowers in your own front yard. If you're renting, you probably won't bother. That's the way our people feel about their business. They own it, so they take care of it."

Patrice Nagasawa said, "I want the customer to think of *me* as being Nordstrom. I believe the Bellevue Square Savvy department is *my* franchise. This company gives you the freedom to help the customer with everything. No one tells you that there's only one way to do your business. Nordstrom lets you do whatever it takes to make the customer happy, as long as it's legal. They are not going to say 'no' to you if the end result is a happy customer."

Knowing they will receive full credit when things go well and full blame when they don't, real Nordies enjoy the freedom that comes from operating under the store's single rule: *Use your good judgment in all situations.*

"I would never be comfortable in an environment where there are a lot of rules," said Van Mensah, of the men's clothing department in the Pentagon City, Virginia, store in suburban Washington, D.C., who sold $1 million worth of merchandise in 1994, working ten months of the year.

"What we resist like crazy is making a rule because one person made a mistake. Then everybody has to live by a rule because one person did something they shouldn't have done," said Wikstrom. "Get those rules out of the way because all you get are people who are paralyzed. Companies say they are empowering their workers. But when you ask to see their employee handbook, they show you a 400-page manual. Who's going to do anything if they are afraid they are going to break the rules?"

Because Nordstrom doesn't have a lot of rules, "we don't have to worry whether we're breaking them," said Annette Armony. Associates are judged on their performance, not their obedience to orders. Armony recalled the time when a customer in her department misplaced a shopping bag containing three bars of soap that had been purchased in the lingerie department. "I went over to lingerie and got three more bars of soap and gave them to her. She thanked me and said, 'I can't believe you did this.'" The bars of soap were only 90¢ apiece, but they produced a happy customer.

Individual creativity is a byproduct of that freedom. Leslie Kaufman, who sells men's clothing at the Westside Pavilion in Los Angeles, left a teaching career because retail "allowed me to still be creative and use my best salesmanship qualities." Dressing her gentleman customers is "not any different than being a painter. I put a personal touch to every customer I serve. There are men who depend on me, who call me at the store and ask me to pick out three suits and all the shirts and ties to go with them. There's a wonderful sense of pride and ego attached to that," said Kaufman, who grew up in a retailing family. "You can be as creative and inventive as you want in developing a clientele. If I were operating a free-standing shop on Rodeo Drive with my name on it, I wouldn't be operating it any differently."

For almost a decade, Los Angeles businessman Robert Fisher has been a Kaufman customer. He considered

Kaufman's close collaboration with Ermanno Cavoto, the master tailor in her department, "very integral to this relationship because Leslie cultivates Ermanno's efforts to serve me," said Fisher, managing partner of Wertheim Schroder & Co., the Los Angeles-based U.S. affiliate of Schroders PLC, the British merchant bank. (Nordstrom has tailor shops in all of its full-line stores.)

Clearly, working at Nordstrom is not for everybody. "That's what we try to tell people who want to work at Nordstrom," said Marty Wikstrom. (The company receives hundreds of job applications each day.) We tell them that our company is all about selling. Sometimes people want to come to work here but they don't like to sell; they don't want to sell. So, every single day they come in here to work, they are under a lot of pressure, because they are doing something that's not natural to them, not fun, not interesting, and not stimulating. It's pressure. Most people who are good at sales are energized by it. They love it. They love the freedom with the customer. They love to work with the customer. They are expressive and they have a lot of fun on the selling floor. They look forward to getting there and making it happen."

Success at Nordstrom "depends on your personality and how much you like being around people," said Sally Eustis, a former Nordstrom sales associate, buyer, and manager. "Some people find it challenging and respond to it; others find it too scary to handle." The ones who don't last are unable to maintain a high level of competence in customer service and sales performance. "You can work at Nordstrom for a few years, but sooner or later, your bad habits will defeat you," said McCarthy.

The company has very high expectations, "and if you don't make it, you're out of there," said Betsy Sanders, the former vice-president of the California division. "People would ask me if it was true that if you don't do a good job at Nordstrom you're gone. I'd say, 'Yes, I hope so.' This is not civil service. It's hard work; there are pressures and expectations." That thought was echoed by Annette Armony: "If you don't care about the customer and how you really want to serve her, you're not going to last very long." The annual turnover rate of salespeople is about 23 percent.

"Some people who work at Nordstrom may find that they are in the wrong job," said McCarthy. "If sales aren't for you, but you like the company, Nordstrom will find a place for you as a support person. We don't want to lose people who have been with the company for several years, because they understand the culture."

Nevertheless, Wikstrom said, "We always say, 'you're performance is your review. It's your interview to your next job.' I always find it fascinating when people say, 'I'm really bad at *this* job, but if I could just get that other job, I'd be really good at it." But, if you haven't done the first job well, how do I know you can do the other job?"

After the first ninety days of employment, associates discuss their job performance in an informal one-on-one session with their manager. Salespeople are evaluated on three criteria—productivity, customer service, and team play—that are all weighed equally. If the associate is not selling, the department manager will make recommendations, such as ways of making better use of his or her personal book or teaming up with an experienced associate who knows how to assemble a personal book and can provide some individual assistance.

From the time Joe Dover, who sells men's shoes in the Seattle-area Bellevue Square store, joined Nordstrom in 1979, he had earned awards, promotions, and responsibility, working his way up to men's shoe buyer, and "enjoying myself tremendously," he recalled. But when he became a shoe buyer at the Southcenter Mall store in Seattle, he ran into a position that was "over my head. The store manager and I didn't click." Dover was fired. "The store manager opened my eyes that I wasn't learning and growing. To be told that I wasn't what Nordstrom's men's shoes wanted really put a bug in me. Instead of saying, 'I'll show them; I'll go elsewhere to make my mark,' I was determined to make it back and I didn't care how long it took." Dover talked his way into helping out in the shoe stockroom during the Half-Yearly Sale and then a month later during the Anniversary Sale as a part-time shoe salesperson. "I convinced them to hire me back because my sales were so good." That was almost a decade ago and he's been a Pacesetter ever since. In hindsight, Dover viewed his firing as "the best thing that happened to me."

Dover is fiercely loyal to the Nordstrom way: "In this era of the discount department store and the bad reputation that salespeople have, there is a group of us here at Nordstrom who really enjoy being salespeople," he said. "We take it seriously and are very happy with that environment. The salesperson position is a good one. It's been a great life for me. There aren't that many $40,000 a year shoe salesmen out there. It's also given me the freedom to take care of my family."

■ The Battle With the Union: A Case Study

This entrepreneurial, do-what-ever-it-takes mindset is incompatible with the bureaucratic, clock-punching mentality of stores where the sales staff is not on commission. What sets Nordstrom apart from the competition "is that if you dedicate yourself to do the little extras, you'll reap the benefits," said Art Langelotti of the Paramus store. "When you come home after work, you're exhausted, but you stay up a little longer to write thank-you notes to customers and birthday cards to their wives and children. If I'm scheduled to come into the store at 1 PM, I'll show up earlier to write thank-you notes because it's quieter than doing it at home when my kids are running around." Langelotti felt that the people who don't make it at Nordstrom fall down on the customer service mentality; "They're not doing the follow-through that goes with it. When six o'clock comes around, they say, 'Good-bye, I'm not going to think about Nordstrom until ten o'clock tomorrow morning.' This is not a nine-to-five job."

In the late 1980s, a clash of basic values had been brewing for years between Nordstrom's top entrepreneurs and the leadership of the two local chapters of the United Food and Commercial Workers Union (UFCW), Local 1001, which represented workers in the five Seattle-area stores, and Local 367, which represented one store in Tacoma. The approximately 1,600 sales associates worked in the only unionized stores in the Nordstrom chain and accounted for less than 5 percent of Nordstrom's total nationwide workforce. The conflict between Nordstrom and the UFCW locals boiled down to a single, philosophical question: *Can Nordstrom's free-wheeling system co-exist with a union frame of mind?* What ensued was a highly publicized battle that questioned the very essence of the Nordstrom system and became the darkest episode in company history since the day Everett and Elmer bought the two-store operation from their father on the eve of the Great Depression.

For corporate executives in any industry, the episode is a case study of employer-union politics, media manipulation, corporate crisis management, and the ultimate triumph of the risk-taker over the risk-foresaker.

Nordstrom had been a union shop for more than sixty years, dating back to the days of John W. Nordstrom and Carl Wallin. This was typical of Seattle, which has a rich history of being one of the most highly unionized cities in the country, dating as far back as 1919, when local workers held the first and only general strike in United States history. At the time, a Seattle businessman ran a newspaper advertisement that railed against "the most labor-tyrannized city in America." (The city was also the home of Dave Beck, the powerful and outspoken president of the International Brotherhood of Teamsters, from 1952 to 1957, when he was succeeded by Jimmy Hoffa.) The Nordstrom brothers, who came from a working-class background themselves, had always felt that, "unions did a lot of good for employees by fighting for higher wages, shorter hours, and more fringe benefits," recalled Elmer. "This was especially true back in the old days when some stores barely paid a living wage." Nordstrom had maintained relatively peaceful relations with its unions, with the exception of an eleven-day strike in 1954. But ever since the 1930s, the company's pay scale, which was traditionally higher than the competition, placed Nordstorm on the front line in contract negotiations. "The union figured that if we could be compelled to raise wages, then they could go to the other stores and say, 'You better raise your wages. Just look at the contract we signed with Nordstrom's,'" recalled Elmer. Up through the 1980s, Nordstrom continued to set the wage standard for Seattle retail workers.

The seeds of Nordstrom's struggle with the UFCW were sown in 1987. On the eve of new contract talks, many employees had asked Nordstrom management to request that the new contract include optional membership, which would have made Nordstrom, in the union vernacular, an "open shop." Those employees saw no advantage to being the only Nordstrom sales associates paying union dues (twenty-four dollars a month for full-time employees; fifteen a month for part-timers). "We couldn't see any benefit or value in what the union was doing," said McCarthy. "The union was in the stores once a year, when the contract negotiations were coming up. The union outlived its usefulness. If Nordstrom did something to me that I thought was unfair, I would be protected under today's laws. But even more important, Nordstrom has always had an open-door policy. If you have a problem, you take it to your department manager. If you can't get satisfaction, you go to your store manager or the regional vice-president, and finally to the Nordstroms themselves."

In July 1987, Nordstrom associates agreed to a twenty-six-month contract. Wages ranged from $8.88 to $10.50 an hour, the highest in the city. Joe Peterson, the president of Local 1001, told the *Seattle Times* that it would have taken a strike to change the company's proposal, but that a strike was not in the members' best interests. Peterson knew that the members would not have voted for a strike. As he later told the *Seattle Times*, "Nordstrom has always been the weakest of our units. Traditionally, many Nordstrom employees have been more loyal to the company than to the union." Or as *Seattle Weekly* quoted one non-union associate: "I don't think Joe understands that a lot of people here like working for Nordstrom." Evidence that most Nordstrom associates considered the union irrelevant (other than the dues they were compelled to pay) was that less than 15 percent of the estimated 1,600 local union members bothered to vote for the new contract.

That confrontation set the stage for what was to happen two years later, when the contract was up again for negotiation in July 1989. A key issue that emerged at that time was Nordstrom's policy of scheduling work hours, which rewarded the best shifts based on productivity rather than seniority—unlike the other major Seattle retailers, The Bon Marche and Frederick & Nelson. To true Nordies, scheduling based on seniority rather than productivity was contradictory to this system. Nordstrom's decentralized managers have the freedom to schedule associates according to subjective criteria such as desire to give customer service and being a "team player," and the more objective measure of sales-per-hour performance. (For example, Nordstrom expects full-time workers to sell a minimum average of $140.74 worth of merchandise per hour; the average varies by department.) The union charged that managers used the scheduling system to play favorites. But under the Nordstrom system, managers' favorites are generally the sales associates that make their department the most money.

The union also alleged that the emphasis on sales performance forced managers to compel employees to work extra hours for "non-selling" business and support activities—writing thank-you notes, stocking inventory, attending meetings, and delivering merchandise to customers or to other stores—and to not record those hours, which would have been a violation of Washington state wage-and-hour laws. By that scenario, an employee who logged only sales time would have a higher sales-per-hour ratio than a co-worker who clocked all other hours. (Oddly, the question of off-the-clock work never once surfaced in the collective bargaining process at Nordstrom or any other retailers with UFCW contracts.)

"The union basically said, 'There's too much pressure, which creates a difficult and unpleasant work environment,'" said Bruce Nordstrom. "Well, to some people, there's no question that that's true, but to the

Pat McCarthys of the world, it's a fabulous environment. That's exactly what they want, and they would be bored to tears and very unproductive if they didn't have that environment. So I think it depends on who you are. We're not for everybody; there's no question about it. But I think now there's more pressure on all of us. Do we rise to it or not? It's as simple as that."

Initially, at least, the off-the-clock issues were secondary to the request by Nordstrom (again in response to requests by many sales associates) that optional union membership be included in the new contract. The union insisted that the proposal be taken off the table because an open shop would surely strip the union of its Nordstrom membership (and their total annual dues of approximately $1.5 million). When Nordstrom refused to drop the proposal, the union felt it was faced with "the major challenge of our history," said Peterson. The union was "fighting for its survival. If Nordstrom was successful in getting rid of its union, there would be every other employer wanting to do the same thing," Peterson told *Women's Wear Daily.* The two sides dug in and began a battle in the courts, the media, and the court of public opinion. The scope of this battle was something that Nordstrom was not prepared for. "We told them they would pay the price," said Peterson, who was no stranger to Nordstrom. A former shoe clerk in the downtown Seattle store, his mother was a part-time Nordstrom salesperson from 1971 to 1978. He was fired by the company in 1975 for honoring a picket line set up by Nordstrom display workers during a one-day strike. He was later reinstated after a ruling by the National Labor Relations Board (NLRB). A couple of years later, he became a professional unionist and in 1986 was elected president of the local.

The union's strategy was to attack Nordstrom's greatest strength and most fragile commodity—its reputation—with a negative publicity offensive. In a letter to John Nordstrom, Larry Kenney, president of the Washington State Labor Council, threatened the company with "a national campaign aimed at your customers, board members, and business associates, targeting every aspect of the company's operations—from development and construction to procurement and retailing." The campaign began in July 1989, timed to coincide with Nordstrom's popular Anniversary Sale, when tuxedo-clad union representatives (few or none of them actual Nordstrom employees, depending on which side's story you believe) handed out shopping bags at six local Nordstrom stores with this message: "Thanks to all our customers from the union members of Nordstrom."

After the contract expired in July 1989, Nordstrom was no longer obliged to provide the union with the names of new hires. Previously, all new employees had been required to join the union and to immediately begin paying dues. *Ipso facto*, Nordstrom had become an open shop.

That wasn't the union's only worry. A group of employees operating under the name Nordstrom Employees Opposed to Union Representation (NEOUR) was working on decertifying Local 1001. (The National Labor Relations Board could order a decertification election if more than 30 percent of employees petitioned for it or if the company had evidence that more than 30 percent of members didn't want the union.)

NEOUR was opposed to the union in general and the union's negative publicity campaign against Nordstrom in particular. "We felt that Nordstrom wasn't being treated fairly by the union and by the media," said Joe Dover, who organized NEOUR with John Rockwood, who was then a shoe salesperson in the company's downtown Seattle store; Kathleen Sargeant, men's furnishings, downtown Seattle; and Diane Aldrich, men's suits at Northgate. "We were seeing a one-sided picture of the issue, of Nordstrom as labor-abuser and Nordstrom employees not happy with their jobs. We chose to speak up and say that we were happy employees. It became obvious very early on to those of us in the system that Joe Peterson lost touch with the desires of the Nordstrom employees. (Over 50 percent of the current employees had been at Nordstrom for less than two and a half years.) He was not out to help Nordstrom employees. The campaign was never voted on by Nordstrom employees. He never called a meeting of Nordstrom employees to discuss how the union was going to handle the negotiations because he knew we would reject it."

NEOUR held rallies in Bellevue and Seattle (the latter drew more than 900 people), and joined forces with employees who held rallies at Nordstrom stores in San Francisco, southern California, and Washington, D.C. NEOUR and other anti-union associates demonstrated in front of the stores, carrying signs reading "We Love Our Company" and wearing "Nobody Asked Us" buttons. In Seattle, more than 1,000 employees signed an ad that said, "We are proud to work for Nordstrom. We support our company and the atmosphere of excellence it fosters." In Orange County, workers ran similar ads (and pointed out that the $3,500 cost was paid for entirely through voluntary contributions from over 1,100 Nordstrom employees in the region). "We had to take money out of our own pockets and we were off the selling floor trying to do this," said Dover. "People thought the Nordstrom family was feeding us money to do this but we didn't get anything directly from them."

NEOUR collected 800 decertification signatures in less than one week's time, but the petition was disallowed because NLRB regulations prohibited a decertification vote while there were still unresolved charges filed by the union. The NLRB ruled that Nordstrom managers violated federal labor laws by illegally assisting some of its employees in the decertification effort, including paying employees for collecting signatures for the petition while on company time; giving employees time off to attend a pro-company rally; allowing decertification meetings on company premises; and allowing anti-union material to be posted on company bulletin boards, while denying similar access to pro-union members. In a bit of pretzel bureaucratic logic, the NLRB admitted that it "did not find that as a general proposition the employer had funded the decertification" and "looking at this thing piece by piece, it doesn't amount to much. But when you add it all up, it amounts to something."

"The decertification vote," Peterson said at that time, "is just not going to happen."

In early 1990, the Washington State Department of Labor & Industry claimed that Nordstrom had violated state law in five areas: failing to pay employees for all company meetings they attended; failing to keep pertinent employment records; failing to pay all hours worked delivering merchandise, writing thank-you notes, and stocking shelves; and miscalculating overtime wages. Nordstrom was asked to compensate all current and former employees and to comply with record-keeping provisions. Nordstrom argued that it had been following compensation practices that were well established in the Washington state retail industry, and that following that system, overtime pay had been traditionally computed according to federal wage standards. (The company later

learned that the state of Washington had allowed for a
different interpretation of how to calculate overtime,
which the Department of Labor & Industry had previously approved for other industries. Eventually, the King
County Superior Court dismissed these claims.)

Nordstrom's bonus plan for managers is based, in part,
on their holding down their selling costs, which are directly related to the number of hours that sales associates
record on their timecards. The company found that some
lower-level managers did, in fact, pressure employees into
performing duties off the clock and did not pay them for
attending meetings. This practice was "against company
policy," co-chairman Jack McMillan told *Women's Wear
Daily*, but, "we are responsible for the pressure of middle
managers. We want our selling costs controlled. One way
to control selling costs—not the right way—is to encourage
people to get the work done in a certain time frame. If they
can't get it done, then there is implied pressure to work off
the clock."

McMillan reflected that the best thing to come out of
the situation was that "people now know we are human."

The company set up a claims process to deal with
complaints of off-the-clock work. Pay practices were
changed and a new policy was laid out for employees to
record all hours worked. Nordstrom immediately began
paying workers for attending store meetings, inventory
work, and making "hand carries"—picking up merchandise at one store and delivering it to another. If done
during regular work hours, hand carries would be covered as part of an employee's selling hours, which determine sales-per-hour performance. Recording these
additional hours would be a disincentive for top salespeople because vacation pay is determined by sales-per-
hour results. Other deliveries that were made to help the
department would be considered "non-sell" hours, and

would not affect sales-per-hour performance. (Employees would receive their hourly wage rate for that time.) When making deliveries going to or from work, pay would be calculated over and above the regular commute time. The same criteria would apply to an associate's delivery to a customer's home, office, or hotel. The Nordstrom rule book was expanded, at least metaphorically, by a few pages.

Many enterprising sales associates disagree in principle with being paid specifically for deliveries made to their personal customers. "Customer service means being there when the customer needs you," said Annette Armony. "I sometimes deliver things to a customer who is disabled. That's part of my job. Our structure gives us more flexibility with the customer, and the payoff is always going to be there. Without my personal customers, I wouldn't be making the money I do." As an example, Armony cited one typical day when she went out of her way—by her own choice—to help several customers. Before her shift began, Armony drove to another Portland-area Nordstrom to pick up a dress for a customer who had to attend a funeral and then drove back several miles to the Washington Square store, where she handed the garment to the deeply appreciative client. Later that day, Armony delivered a dress to another customer, who needed it by a certain time and couldn't get to the store. Those kinds of heroics "make Nordstrom look even better in the customer's eyes."

Nordstrom set aside $15 million for back-pay claims and immediately paid about $3 million to approximately 4,000 out-of-state employees. Under the Nordstrom plan, $1,000 in back pay would be given to employees with nineteen or more months service; $750 to employees with thirteen to nineteen months; $500 for seven to thirteen months and $300 for employment for three to seven months.

Peterson told *Women's Wear Daily* that the $15 million was "wholly inadequate." He contended that the biggest claim received by the union was for $20,000; with the average claim being for about $4,000 and that "we estimate that in Washington alone, Nordstrom's liabilities could be between $30 million and $40 million; in California, in excess of $200 million." This was an overstatement because Nordstrom's *total selling payroll* in 1989 was $300 million. It would be the first of many times that Peterson would make exaggerated estimates of Nordstrom's potential liability. Peterson later charged that if the lawsuit was successful, it would result in the largest liabilities ever paid out by any employer for violation of wage and hour laws. By this time, he was claiming that Nordstrom could owe as much $1.4 billion. In fact, at the end of 1990, a King County Superior Court judge rebuked the UFCW for misleading Nordstrom workers over facts surrounding the lawsuit, specifically that the union local's newsletter "strongly implie(d)" that employees who joined the suit would get a minimum of $7,000 in damages, when no amount had been established.

Not surprisingly, Nordstrom was soon the target of a class action suit filed on behalf of shareholders who had purchased stock between February 1, 1989, and February 15, 1990. They alleged that the company and five of its principal officers knew, or should have known, that the unpaid work and overtime claims by employees would adversely impact the price of the company stock and that the company should have made a disclosure to that effect. The suit was later settled out of court, with Nordstrom forced to pay those shareholders $5 million. That settlement contributed to a disappointing 1989 for Nordstrom, whose profits declined for the first time since the company went public in 1970. Sales grew by 15 percent to $2.67

billion, but profits slid 6.8 percent to $115 million, due in part to the $15 million reserve for back-pay claims and litigation.

The union kept filing unfair labor practice lawsuits wherever Nordstrom did business. For example, the national UFCW asked the Virginia Department of Labor to investigate whether Nordstrom violated the rights of sales clerks at the East Coast store. The union local sent a newsletter to brokerage houses and retail analysts outlining problems it claimed the company would face as a result of the litigation. During the holiday shopping season, a union worker (not a Nordstrom employee), dressed as Santa Claus, handed out anti-Nordstrom leaflets in front of Nordstrom stores. "We are using the Chinese water drop torture method," said Peterson, who was hoping to unionize the rest of Nordstrom's stores.

In March 1990, the UFCW filed a class action lawsuit against Nordstrom on behalf of 50,000 past and present employees in Washington, Oregon, California, Alaska, Utah, and Virginia. The allegations were that Nordstrom discouraged employees from submitting claims for all time worked and threatened reprisals if they did submit claims; "compelled, coerced, or required" employees to buy and wear Nordstrom clothing at work; and improperly subtracted commissions from employees for returns on merchandise that were not originally sold by the employee whose commission was affected. (Nordstrom accepts all returns of merchandise no matter how much time has passed between the original purchase and the return. The company policy is to deduct the same commission on a return as was earned by the employee on the original sale.)

Meanwhile, Peterson was a one-man traveling press conference, answering every media inquiry and appearing on radio talk shows and in front of television cameras at virtually every opportunity. The negative publicity campaign, which was financed by the national UFCW and run by a Washington, D.C., consulting group, was brilliant. The stories that were generated in publications such as the *Los Angeles Times, Investor's Daily,* the *San Francisco Examiner,* and *Time* magazine positioned the battle primarily from the union's point of view because the union was the more aggressive in telling its side of the story. Nordstrom had grossly underestimated what Peterson was capable of doing. As the *Seattle Post-Intelligencer* reported, when the controversy first "began to unfold, Nordstrom officials . . . took a routine and cautious approach to telling their side of the story, using terse, carefully worded press releases or opting not to comment on the union's charges." This was a serious mistake because Nordstrom didn't immediately grasp that it was involved in a political campaign that was going to be played out in the court of public opinion. It is a cardinal rule of politics that if you don't define yourself, your opponent will do it for you.

After a seemingly unrelenting series of negative articles in the local Seattle papers, the Nordstroms finally lost their collective temper. The company announced it was going to dramatically cut back its advertising in the *Seattle Times* and the *Seattle Post-Intelligencer*—where they had combined annual expenditures of about $1.5 million a year—and redirect those dollars to radio and television. In an interview on a Seattle radio station, Jim Nordstrom blasted the print coverage as "biased" and "unconscionable," but claimed that the decision to reduce print advertising was strictly business, based on a poor return for their advertising dollar. But even if that was the case, the timing was poor, the pique was obvious, and Nordstrom did not help its case in the court of public opinion. A typical reaction came from a local public relations executive who told *Seattle Weekly* (although not for attribution) that Nordstrom's move was a "combination of arrogance and ignorance."

Nordstrom would later get professional public relations assistance, but not before it was hit by the most devastating and damaging newspaper story of all. On the morning of February 20, 1990, *Wall Street Journal* readers were greeted with this headline over the lead front page story: "At Nordstrom Stores, Service Comes First—But at a Big Price." The story, written by staff reporter Susan C. Faludi, described a dark, Dickensian tale of "Nervous Nordies"—products of a "dysfunctional" family, who suffered from "ulcers, colitis, hives, and hand tremors." She conceded that "no doubt, thousands of salespeople have thrived in the Darwinian struggle on the sales floor," and quoted Pat McCarthy, who proudly described his position at Nordstrom as "a people job, which I love." Still, she was clearly irked by the Nordstrom way, including the fact that sales clerks were expected to occasionally empty the trash.

The *Journal* story contained many inaccuracies. For example, Nordstrom's success was credited, in part, to "low labor costs," although, in fact, Nordstrom has some of the highest labor costs in retail because it has more salespeople on the floor. A former cosmetics salesperson claimed to be consistently one of her department's top performers, but in some years, she said, she made only $18,000. (Nordstrom's top cosmetics salespeople make $30,000 or more.) And one person who was identified as a "former employee" never worked at Nordstrom.

In the article, Sean Mulholland, a salesman in a Seattle-area Nordstrom store, claimed that he was fired because he had contracted the AIDS virus. He further asserted that the had attempted 16 times in 18 months to apply for jobs that were posted at four Nordstrom stores in the area and "was always turned away." As proof, Mulholland claimed that he had saved copies of the rejection letters he received from Nordstrom managers.

Nordstrom contended that Mulholland's department manager had initially expressed concern to the store manager that Mulholland hadn't been coming to work; had never given specific reasons for his absences; and had never returned phone calls. With a big sale coming up, the manager needed to know whether she could count on Mulholland, who, according to Nordstrom records, had a history of calling in late or asking someone to cover for him, without talking directly to his manager. Mulholland finally came in for a private talk with the store manager and department manager, who asked if there was a physical or emotional problem that caused him to miss work. At that point, he allegedly broke down and explained that he had tested positive for the AIDS virus. The store manager later told Nordstrom investigators that she responded to that information by hugging Mulholland, expressing her sorrow, and promising that the information would remain confidential. She asked him if he was strong enough to continue to work the sales floor. He said he wasn't, but indicated that he still wanted to work for Nordstrom. The store manager told him he had several options, including lighter work and medical leave. She suggested that he think about it and let her know within a few days. While several people tried to find Mulholland another position, he never followed up. Nevertheless, the company continued to pay for his medical coverage.

James Nordstrom wrote to *The Wall Street Journal* with a point-by-point rebuttal of the Faludi story, including her misrepresentation of the Mulholland episode, but the newspaper refused to print his letter and stuck by the story. The San Francisco bureau chief, who supervised Faludi, was quoted in the *Seattle Post-Intelligencer* as saying that Mulholland "has copies of sixteen rejection letters, and so has Susan." But when *Wall Street Journal* deputy managing editor Paul E. Steiger later asked Faludi to check again, the result was different. In a May 7, 1990, letter to Jim Nordstrom, Steiger wrote: "It turns out that we erred when we asserted Mr. Mulholland had letters from Nordstrom rejecting his request to return to work. . . . We now understand him to say that he kept a written record of what he says were his sixteen rejections, not that he had sixteen written rejections from Nordstrom." The *Journal* printed a one-and-a-half-inch correction. Not surprisingly, the Mulholland episode inspired protests: several hundred demonstrators from the AIDS Coalition to Unleash Power (ACT UP) marched in front of the downtown San Francisco store,

In fact, Mulholland had not been Nordstrom's first employee with AIDS. At that time, Nordstrom knew of an estimated two dozen employees who had contracted HIV. The company had spent over $400,000 on medical care, donated over $100,000 to AIDS charities, adjusted work schedules and total hours to accommodate health limitations, and brought in health experts to explain the disease to co-workers and to answer questions. Around the time of *The Wall Street Journal* story, a terminally ill Nordstrom employee had been flown home, at company expense, to spend his final days with his parents.

Two years earlier, in the summer of 1988, Ralph Bisdale, a Nordstrom lighting display designer, had contracted the virus. According to Bisdale's supervisor, Barden Erickson (the former Nordstrom director of store planning), Bisdale continued to receive full pay—even when he could no longer work—until he died in April

1990. In his last days, Bisdale wrote letters to the *Seattle Times, Seattle Post-Intelligencer,* and the *Wall Street Journal* that defended Nordstrom's treatment of employees with HIV. "When I told my manager about my problems, there was no change in the way I was treated except in a favorable way," Bisdale wrote. "I was given whatever time I needed off. I work in the AIDS community when I can, and every care giver and volunteer who knows people with AIDS has remarked to me that no one treats their people with AIDS better than Nordstrom." Bisdale died a few months later. None of the papers printed the letter.

What are we to make of *The Wall Street Journal* article? Writing in the December 11, 1990, issue of *Financial World,* Jude Wanniski, a former editorial writer for the *Journal* called it "one of the most biased business reports in *Journal* history."

A different approach was taken by *60 Minutes,* which, during the height of the controversy, went to Seattle to find out what was going on between the retailer and its union. Correspondent Morley Safer and *60 Minutes* investigators interviewed Bruce, John, and James Nordstrom and Jack McMillan, and also spoke with Joe Peterson and James Webster (the attorney representing UFCW) and a cross-section of employees for the May 5, 1990, segment, entitled "The Nordstrom Boys."

Webster charged that "the horror stories of the twenties are present at Nordstrom today" and Peterson said that even if top Nordstrom sales associates considered themselves professionals, "The fact is, the law says they are clock punchers."

Diane Aldrich visibly surprised Safer with the comment that Nordstrom sales associates "do not need outside influences breeding mediocrity and subjugating people." And regarding the off-the-clock charges, Aldrich added, "I've never been asked to work overtime, or make deliveries, or do anything I didn't feel in my heart I wanted to do for many reasons, and my paycheck reflects that service I give. Everything I do I am compensated for in many many ways." Such loyalty, Safer conceded with a wry expression on his face, "may be hard to understand, but it's genuine."

Marti Galovic Palmer, who produced the Nordstrom segment for *60 Minutes*, was given a list of people to interview by Local 1001. "A lot of what I was looking for in terms of hard complaints turned out to be from people who just wanted a job that didn't demand a whole lot," she recalled. "Basically, their attitude was 'It's a nice place to work, I like the job, but I don't want it to consume my life.' In the end, it was a little hard to get around that with a lot of the people that the union sent us to." On the other hand, Palmer and her associates interviewed—on their own—many other salespeople who were "incredibly energetic and wanted it to consume their life."

For Nordstrom, what was riding on the *60 Minutes* interview?

"Our credibility was at stake; that's all," said Bruce Nordstrom. "If *60 Minutes* wanted to take advantage of us, they could have. This was happening right at the absolute depth of this whole [union] episode. We were fighting and scratching and we thought we were being treated very unfairly by various media. But Morley Safer prevailed upon us. He convinced us that they would be fair. I was impressed with the homework they did. They spent two weeks in Seattle before the interview, talking to people. To their credit, they presented the story straight. That was a real turning point in the public relations battle." The irony for Nordstrom was that the media that savaged it ultimately brought it to salvation.

Ten days after the *60 Minutes* segment aired, Nordstrom had its annual shareholders' meeting in Newport Beach, California. During the meeting, which the *Seattle Post-Intelligencer* said, "took on the air of a political convention," employees spoke on both sides of the issue. Peterson was in attendance to give interviews but not to speak during the meeting.

A subdued Bruce Nordstrom spoke for the entire corporation and the Nordstrom family about the sting of the public relations campaign. The union charges and the resulting bad publicity "have disturbed us and our families deeply, both personally and professionally." But he was still unbowed. "Make no mistake," he continued. "Freedom is the issue, not just freedom to belong or not belong to a union, but freedom to wait on customers in the best way, freedom to go the extra mile, freedom to pursue a career in sales or in management, freedom to make customer service decisions right there on the sales floor without a lot of silly rules and interference, and freedom from being called 'clock punchers' as they have been by this union's management." After briefly retelling the company history, he said that "three generations of Nordstroms have done our best to hold to the legacy passed along by our grandpa and his dreams. So don't think for a moment that we will abandon the fundamental retailing principles that have served your company through our first eighty-nine years. To the contrary, we want to see those principles alive and thriving for the next eighty-nine years, and with your support, we will."

In July, the workers in the five Seattle-area stores voted to decertify the union by a vote of 1,022 to 407. This time, Nordstrom played hardball. During the decertification campaign, the company set up a twenty-four-hour telephone hotline and produced three anti-union videos—

two shown at staff meetings; the third was mailed to workers' homes at company expense. Two videos featured Nordstrom family members urging employees to vote for the company's position. The third consisted of actors portraying pro-company and pro-union employees discussing the decertification vote with a new employee. A year later, the Tacoma local 367 voluntarily left the Tacoma store in anticipation of being decertified. "We were successful because we were dedicated to the principle that Nordstrom customer service was at stake and we didn't want to lose it," said Joe Dover. "In many cases, unions are still viable, but when you lose sight of what the employees want, you're lost."

Even *The Wall Street Journal* came around. "The point is that Nordstrom attracts and rewards a special type of employee, and the rest of us should punch in elsewhere," wrote columnist Tim W. Ferguson. "That wasn't good enough for the UFCW. Competitors can be expected to mimic the act (and have been trying to). Before long, workers will be getting a taste of what many an entrepreneur has learned, that you're never really master of your own destiny, but somewhat servile to your customer."

On January 11, 1993, the UFCW's class action lawsuit ended in an out-of-court settlement. Current and former Nordstrom employees who worked at least 200 regular hours between February 16, 1987, and March 15, 1990, were eligible to file claims for off-the-clock wage compensation. Commissioned sales personnel received three hours pay for every 100 hours worked during the period for a total of up to $2,000. Noncommissioned personnel received 1.2 hours' pay for every 100 hours worked. Overtime wages were paid to eligible class members employed during the period from February 16, 1987, to September

15, 1992. The total outlay was for considerably less than
Peterson's most conservative estimate. Nordstrom paid out
approximately $5 million under the settlement, with a me-
dian payout of $170. Only 1,444 people received checks
for more than $1,000. Several people received about
$7,000. All of them had worked in one department in one
state, where the method of calculating overtime had been
done incorrectly, not only by Nordstrom, but by other
stores as well. About 1,900 checks were for less than
$10.00. "We were paying the union protection money," said
Pat McCarthy. "What we got back from the settlement were
some of the dues we had been paying over the years."

The big payoff went to the union's attorneys: legal fees
and costs of administering the settlement reportedly
came to about $6.6 million.

Reflecting on this episode, the Nordstroms readily conceded that Joe Peterson was an effective advocate for his
side. "I give him all the credit in the world for catching us
off guard," said Jim Nordstrom. His brother John agreed:
"We knew that we were in a fight with somebody that had
nothing to lose. But we're pretty stubborn, and we knew
that once we got into it, we were going to go to the end of
the earth to win it. There were many times, I suppose,
when somebody else would have said, 'To hell with this;
I'm not going to put up with this anymore.' I think that's
what the union was counting on, but it didn't happen.
They thought, because we were so proud of our company,
that we would cave in, but we didn't want to pass along
that kind of legacy to the next generation."

In hindsight, how would the Nordstroms have handled the union situation differently?

"That's a great question," Bruce Nordstrom said with a
chuckle. "As you might expect, we've given the whole subject a lot of thought. We've dissected that one over and over

again. There's no question that the pain that we went through was more than we thought we were going to get. As things started to unfold, the real union experts warned us. They said, 'You guys ought to know what you're getting into.' We had been dealing with the union all of our lives. They weren't that strong. We thought it would be unpleasant. We thought that right was right."

What is the Nordstroms' advice to other companies faced with a similar dilemma?

"Understand what you're getting into," said Bruce Nordstrom. "Don't take it lightly because [taking on a union] is a very serious step. It was a very appropriate step for us, and we are much better off today because we went through that pain. But, I'll tell you, the pain was significant. Let the future generations know that if they don't treat people right, they are going to have unions." He did concede that Nordstrom's experience with its union "made us hypersensitive about every facet of the personnel end of our business. I think we're a lot better on minority relations, disabled people, a whole potpourri of subjects. We are building the company stronger because of the sensitivity that they demanded we get." Still, he is thankful the union was decertified because "the negativism is not there any more. That hurts the culture. We want to build up the culture."

After all is said and done, the way the Nordstrom system works is very simple: The people who do the best for the company and themselves are the ones who respond to the system, work the hardest, and do the extra things that it takes to be more productive. Shoe salesman Joe Dover said, "I can't fault those people who say that they need to get paid for doing extra tasks, there's still got to be room to allow salespersons to be the best they can be, to take the initiative to do the extra things. What's wrong with writing thank-you notes at home on your own time or getting the walls stocked to make your area easier to sell in? It will make your income better. I do get paid for that type of work; my commissions prove it. It's ludicrous to be forced to pay someone to sit down and write a thank-you note. How do you make someone be nice to a customer?"

According to co-president Raymond A. Johnson, "we've altered our time-keeping system to account for the writing of thank-you notes. We've taken extraordinary efforts to develop a time-keeping record that accounts for time that they spend promoting their business while not at work."

KEYS TO SUCCESS

Nordstrom tries to hire people who will fit into their system. Some people say Nordstrom employees fall into two categories: (1) exceptional people, and (2) average people who work at an exceptional level because they are supported by the culture. Previous retail experience or a college degree have never been a prerequisite for succeeding at Nordstrom. Because the company assumes that people are best trained by their parents, it provides little in the way of a formalized training program. Workers are sorted out by a natural selection process where only the fittest survive.

- Nordstrom would rather hire nice people and teach them to sell, than hire salespeople and teach them to be nice. Nordstrom, it is said, "hires the smile and trains the skill."
- The best salespeople are entrepreneurial self-starters.
- Nordstrom gives people the freedom to do whatever it takes to make the customer happy (as long as it's legal).
- Real Nordies enjoy the freedom that comes from operating under the store's primary rule: Use your good judgment in all situations.
- Because Nordstrom doesn't have many rules, employees don't have to worry whether they are breaking any.
- Associates are judged on their performance, not their obedience to orders.
- Individual creativity is a by-product of freedom.
- Working at Nordstrom is not for everybody. The company has very high expectations. If you don't meet them, you're gone. Consequently, Nordstrom's entrepreneurial, do-what-ever-it-takes mindset is incompatible with a union structure.

The Art of Selling

Retailing Is a Contact Sport

The astute reader will have noticed that at Nordstrom the priority is on selling, and the key to successful selling is providing outstanding customer service. Nordstrom's best associates have learned how not to "walk" a customer—i.e., not to lose a sale because they couldn't satisfy a customer's desire. They learn that lesson from practice, experience, and commitment. "People often come to Nordstrom thinking this is an easy job. They don't realize it is pretty complex," said Alice Dick, who sells women's apparel in the Washington Square store in Portland. "You have to appreciate where the customer is coming from. She has a reason to be there, and it's up to you to bring that out and to find out how you can help her."

McCarthy said Nordstrom is not just selling clothes and shoes, it's also selling service. "We can convince customers that we are here to serve them—not just to take their money—by making their experience at Nordstrom easy. Sometimes, that means being the concierge. I get all kinds of requests that are not clothes-related. People ask me the name of a good hotel or a nice place to have dinner, or where to get a massage. If I don't have the answer, I'll find out right away. Gas stations don't sell only gas; sometimes they sell directions."

Associates who develop an understanding of customer service the Nordstrom way have taken the time to grasp the intricacies of the system and to customize it to their own personality and talents. "The best salespeople in Nordstrom have found, through trial and error, what they do best," said David Butler of the Tacoma store. "Not everybody can be a Pacesetter, but everybody has certain strengths."

Half the battle in selling is being perceptive enough to read the customer and secure enough to be comfortable with yourself. "Before I sell the product, I have to sell me first," said Leslie Kaufman of the Westside store in Los Angeles. "If the customers don't believe in me, my product doesn't mean anything."

■ Tools of the Selling Trade

All top sales associates rely heavily on the tools that Nordstrom gives them. One of those tools is the personal customer book, which helps them keep track of every customer's name, telephone number, charge account number, sizes, previous purchases, vendor preferences, likes and dislikes, special orders, and any other characteristics, such as being a difficult fit or preferring to shop during sales events. "Everybody in this company needs to have a book like this. It motivates you to keep going for more," said Kazumi Ohara of the Chanel department in downtown Seattle, whose voluminous personal books (she has several because of the magnitude of her clientele) are the company standard. These expandable, looseleaf personal books also contain daily, weekly, and monthly calendars, a daily calendar for Pacesetter goals, a to-do list, and the phone extension for every department in every Nordstrom store in the country. That last item comes in handy when a salesperson is out of an item or a size and needs to call the other stores to find it. Remember: Nordstrom sales people don't want to "walk" the customer.

McCarthy feels it is essential to record all customers' purchases in his personal book because he services so many downtown Seattle businessmen. His client list includes forty attorneys in one law firm, so he has to make sure that two men who work in the same office, or who are likely to run into each other, aren't wearing the same outfit. "You can have as many customers as you want, but you have to take care of each one on an individual basis," he said. "Ninety percent of your new clients come from referrals from current clients who appreciate the job you have done. I don't want to disappoint them by giving bad service." McCarthy ends his first contact with a new customer by swapping business cards and saying, "This was fun for me. Shall we do this again?"

Maintaining a good personal book helps build the trust of your clientele, said Leslie Kaufman. "In the 1980s, if you did not have a personal clientele, you could depend on walk-in traffic to make your paycheck. It's not that way in the 1990s. Because of the economy and the recession, the foot traffic is not the same. My personal clientele is the primary reason I've maintained my business. I'm constantly finding ways to stay in touch with them and get them into the store. At Christmastime or when a customer's birthday is coming up, I send out a note to his wife: 'Did you get Jack his present yet?'" But at the same time, Kaufman does not depend entirely on personal clientele. "I couldn't do the business that I do without new customers. My goal is to meet three new people a day and make one out of three a personal customer."

McCarthy recommends that new sales associates begin to develop their customer service style by starting with the basics: organize and build a system, believe in it, and then execute it. "It's more than thinking positive," said McCarthy. "Positive thinking comes from following simple steps that produce results." McCarthy compares his personal system of customer service to a car engine, whose parts can be taken apart and reassembled. "I work hard at not having to look like I'm working hard. That comes from constantly thinking and planning. I am a much better salesperson now than I was five to fifteen years ago because I'm learning better ways to service the customer. When Larry Bird played basketball for the Boston Celtics, he looked so natural, you would think he must have always played with such skill and confidence. But Larry Bird was once clumsy; he had to work hard to make his play look natural. Larry Bird 'sees' the basketball floor; I 'see' the sales floor."

McCarthy's preparation each day begins virtually with his initial waking thought. "First put yourself in the right frame of mind. I look in the mirror and say, 'Okay, Pat, what do you need to do today? Why are you going to work today, and what do you hope to gain?'" In his early years as a Nordstrom sales associate, McCarthy often found himself discouraged and stuck in what he called a "poor me" attitude. "I'd ask myself, 'Why am I doing all this? Am I making a difference?' But eventually I learned that I don't have time to get depressed." Feelings of discouragement are not uncommon. Shoe salesman David Butler has seen colleagues psych themselves out the moment they walked into the store in the morning and took a look at the previous day's print-out—the evidence of what they sold and what was returned. "They get depressed over the amount of merchandise that was returned. Forget about returns," advised Butler. "Don't dwell on the past. Yesterday is over. Ask yourself: 'What can I do to sell better *today?*'"

Once McCarthy arrives in his department on the second floor of the downtown Seattle store, he is completely focused on the chores of the day. He's already got several projects in progress because "when I'm in motion, I'm much more creative and opportunities are constantly opening up for me. I visualize my tasks completed." As he reviews the merchandise in his department, he memorizes the colors, sizes, and manufacturers on hand, as well as where the gaps might be. "I'm continually writing notes and reviewing the things I have to do for the day, and double checking to make sure they are getting done. One list, for example, might consist of things to get done in the tailor shop; another list consists of people to call. Everywhere I turn, there is something being accomplished. I don't leave things to chance. Things that I planned a week or a month ago are being taken care of. I want to do them right the first time so that I'm free to move on to the next task." He always arrives at the store early in order to tackle the most difficult tasks first, so that they aren't hanging over his head all day. "Don't put things off until the end of the day when you're ready to leave. If I have to call a customer because something wasn't done right, I'll get it out of the way. By doing so, I can start the day fresh and the customer gets the sense that Nordstrom values and cares for its customers. I'm not only building Nordstrom's business, I'm building my business and my relationship with that customer."

■ Dialing for Dollars

The telephone—more specifically, *several* telephones in virtually every department—is one of the most powerful tools that Nordstrom provides associates for generating business and improving productivity. "Some retailers think that providing a telephone is a luxury; Nordstrom thinks it is a basic tool," said Van Mensah of the Pentagon City store, "because there is money sitting on the other end of the line."

The phone is on Mensah's mind when he walks into the store before the start of his 1 PM shift. "I first check out my [men's clothing] area, then I go to the furnishings department to see what new shirts and ties have come in. I make a mental note of what suit will go with them, then I'll call a particular customer and say, 'There is a beautiful tie and shirt that just came in that will go with a lot of things you bought. Do you have time to take a quick look?'" The telephone is especially important to Mensah because he has an international clientele that includes State Department personnel, Pentagon attaches, and corporate executives. He doesn't hesitate calling clients in Portugal or Turkey or Germany to alert them to an upcoming sale, new items that are arriving in the store, gaps in their wardrobes, shoes that need replacement, and so on. (On his days off, Mensah calls overseas customers from his home, via Nordstrom's tie-line long distance phone system.) New customers "are surprised that a salesman will have the access to call overseas. It opens a different line of communication," said Mensah. Making those phone calls in the morning "clears my mind. So, when I'm on the floor, those people who I didn't reach will be calling me back. That's what gets the ball rolling."

McCarthy has found that his phone calls (he generally makes about forty a day) also provide him with information that he can use on the job. "I saw the 1991 recession six months before the economists did because I heard it in my customers' voices and saw it in their buying patterns. When business is tough, people buy for needs, not wants. With that information, when I make my next call, I let the customer know that I understand that today might not be the right time to come in, and that I'll touch base in another month or two. But, I want him to know I'm thinking about him."

McCarthy suggests that sales associates in any business should learn how to use the telephone as a tool. "Give your customer a warm hello—even if you don't feel it. Avoid sounding preoccupied. You may have just found out somebody didn't do the job they had promised and you're upset. But that happened to you, it didn't happen to the customer on the other end of the line. It's okay to acknowledge that you are having a terrible morning; you're only human. You might say, 'Let me get some business out of the way and I'll call you back so that I can devote my full attention to you.'"

Joyce Johnson and her four associates in the couture department of the Corte Madera, California, store "live on our telephones; we look like bookies," she quipped. Johnson contacts her best customers to let them know that she has put aside for them something that just went on sale. "They'll laugh. It makes them feel very comfortable," said Johnson, who worked at a downtown San Francisco boutique for thirteen years before joining Nordstrom in 1988. "I've got nothing to lose by doing it. If they don't like it, fine, but once it goes on sale, it's gone." Johnson doesn't recommend such forwardness with every customer. "You have to know your clientele. I don't do that with people who are stuffy." Top sales associates like Johnson get many of their personal customers by promising to track down an item in the system—and actually *doing* it. Consequently, the phone is essential to customer service "because once our customer crosses the bridge to San Francisco, she is going to have a very large selection. We try to keep her here in Marin County by letting her know that whatever she wants, we can get it for her, if there is any way possible. You do whatever you can to keep the customer happy. If I can't find an item in our system (by calling other Nordstrom stores), I will do a special order or buy outside our system (from a competitor) and put it on my own charge account number. Then the store will reimburse me."

With her telephone in hand, Patrice Nagasawa considers herself in the time-saving business. Several of her best customers rarely venture into the Bellevue Square Savvy department, choosing instead to phone-order merchandise, which she mails out to them. Nagasawa also has many busy "drive-by" customers. "They call me in the morning and tell me what they're looking for; then they call back from their car phone to let me know when they are getting close to Bellevue Square, and again when they're right outside my department, which is near the door. I go outside to show them what I've got, they point out what they want, I run back in the store, ring up the purchases and bring them back out to the customer's car. They drive away, having never set foot in the store. I've developed that trust with these customers because they know I'm not going to abuse it."

■ Earning Customers' Trust

Trust is the coin of the realm at Nordstrom. Customer Vicky LaGrone trusts Patrice Nagasawa to "set aside things that I might like and give me the option to say yes or no before they hit the floor. She seeks them out and finds them for me, which saves me a lot of time. She helps me throughout the store, which saves me more time. My husband and I travel quite a bit. I can say to Patrice, 'We're leaving on a trip in two weeks, this is where we're going, this is what I need.' Patrice knows me well enough to pull it all together."

Many mothers in Portland arrange special appointments for their teenage daughters with Annette Armony of the Brass Plum department "because they trust that I'm not going to put their daughters in a dress that makes them look like Madonna or sell them something they don't want or can't afford. I've built my reputation on that. A teenager has reached that stage where mom is not going to tell her what to wear. So, I play the part of the mediator in order to make them both happy."

Another way for sales associates to earn the confidence of their customers is to be well versed in the merchandise they sell. Product knowledge is Leslie Kaufman's "biggest advantage as a salesperson because I can explain to the customer why the fabric, tailoring, amount of handiwork, etc., determine why one suit costs $1,200 and another $500." Salespeople are required to be thoroughly acquainted with the merchandise, the differences between manufacturers and, perhaps most importantly, where to find the merchandise in the store. They are encouraged to not only try on the merchandise they sell (in order to experience how it feels) but also to buy it and wear it themselves. (McCarthy generally prefers to wear a traditional two-button suit, plain shirt, and regimental-stripe tie, because "most men want their clothing salesman to dress in the middle of the road, and my job is to receive people; not to intimidate them.") Associates in every Nordstrom division are encouraged to keep up with product changes and industry information through seminars, demonstrations, videos, and, occasionally, first-hand looks at how the products are constructed. For example, on the eve of the opening of the Pentagon City store, all of the store's men's clothing sales associates spent an entire day at the factories of the suit manufacturers Norman Hilton and H. Freeman, where they observed the production and learned the companies' design philosophy. "Then you are ready to sell that vendor's clothing," said Van Mensah. David Butler agreed. He recommended that associates "get excited about the product. Too often, salespeople start daydreaming when they are talking to the customer, then they wonder why they didn't sell that shoe. If you're not interested, why would you expect the customer to be interested? Why should I buy something from a sales associate who doesn't care?"

Top associates believe in making customers "your best friends," said Butler. "Treat customers like royalty and let them know that you will take care of them. Customers are here to spend money, so make them happy." Joyce Johnson stressed that she and her co-workers in Corte Madera, are on a first name basis with most of their customers. "We go into the dressing room, have a sparkling water, and just yak about everything—the kids, the vacation. We could be therapists for half our customers because they take us into their confidence. People love to talk about themselves. By the time we get to the merchandise, they're comfortable. Whether you're in retail, real estate, banking, or law, *the idea is to listen to your customer.*"

That sentiment is echoed by Patrice Nagasawa: "The day I stopped worrying about selling and started listening to the customer was the day it all fell into place for me. When you are young and starting out with this company, you want to sell. But the more you talk, and the less you listen, the less you're going to do." Nagasawa's goal is to establish long-term relationships with people that she personally enjoys. "I love the people contact," she said. "Some ladies come in once a week and become very good friends. A lot of salespeople will wait until somebody comes into the department. I look for somebody that I enjoy inviting into the department. I treat them like guests in my living room."

Anne Redman, a Seattle attorney and a longtime Nordstrom customer, said that when she enters the store, "I'm a sixty-pound salmon. There's always something at Nordstrom to hook me. I wander up to a counter and a salesperson pays attention to me. Nordstrom salespeople are enthusiastic and they know what they are selling. When I walk into the store to buy a suit or a pair of shoes or a blouse, I usually walk out with what I want."

■ The Approach

"I believe that 95 percent of the time, when a person comes into the store, they really want to buy," said David Butler. "If you played blackjack in Las Vegas and won 95 percent of the time, you would keep on playing. I like those odds."

When a new customer comes into Nagasawa's department, "I don't rush right over to her, but I always make sure she is acknowledged," said Nagasawa. "I ask her how she is doing today, whether she is looking for something special or a particular size. If she's just looking, I'll invite her to enjoy browsing in the department and to let me know if she has any questions. I try not to wander too far, so that I'm accessible. But I don't hover, because I don't like that when I'm shopping. I want to treat my customers the way I want to be treated. For me, that's it in a nutshell."

Working at Nordstrom, McCarthy said, "forces you to deal with everybody: the good, the bad, and the ugly.

When a customer comes into the department on the defensive or has his own opinions, I give him plenty of room and the opportunity to look over the department on his own. But I still tell him that I am here to help any way I can. The most aggravating customer is the one who doesn't know what he wants and can't reach a decision. I try to get him into a mood where something positive can happen. I might compliment him on the way he dresses and then suggest a manufacturer with a similar style. Or I'll comment that the shading of a particular suit would go well with the color of the shoes he's wearing."

Annette Armony also takes her cues from the customer's attire. When a young woman walks into the Washington Square Brass Plum department, Armony might, for example, suggest a tank top that will go with a color the customer is wearing, or "I'll comment that the shirt she's wearing looks like it's from The Gap, and that we have leggings that would go great with that shirt. That will start a conversation." Armony never simply asks whether she can help the customer because, "You're always going to get a 'no.'"

Although it's important to pick up on what the customer is wearing, sales associates caution that snap judgments that are based on the customers' appearance can be deceiving or worse—they can cause associates to outsmart themselves out of a potentially lucrative sale. For example, when McCarthy was working at the Tacoma store early in his career, a woman in her fifties walked through the sportswear department one morning dressed in tacky clothes and a pair of old white tennis shoes with a hole in the toe. Not surprisingly, there was no stampede of salespeople to wait on her. After a few minutes went by and no one had approached her, McCarthy went over to say hello. Two hours later, she had purchased about $5,000 worth of sport coats, shirts, and sweaters, which, she explained, were uniforms for the crew of her boat. She asked McCarthy to put all the items together for her driver to pick up. The customer turned out to be the daughter of a famous American industrialist, and was on her way to her resort estate in the San Juan Islands of northern Puget Sound. "That was a tremendous learning experience," said McCarthy. "Never judge a book by its cover; open it up. If you treat a kid who is buying a $19.95 belt the same as a businessman buying an $1,995 Oxxford suit, you will be successful. That kid might become a customer for life."

Nordstrom wants to sell everybody. "One of the ongoing cultural truisms, which we have to keep indoctrinating our people in, is that you can't be snooty to customers," said Bruce Nordstrom. "You can't pick and choose who you're going to wait on. You can't say 'this is our customer and this isn't our customer.' They're *all* our customers, and I mean that sincerely. Bring them all in. As long as they spend their money with us, we're going to treat them all the same. The reason why we do so much business per square foot is that we're stretching and reaching out all the time."

That's particularly challenging for McCarthy because he assumes that "every man who comes into the store hates the idea of shopping for clothes and would rather be somewhere else. When he walks into my department for the first time he is surrounded by an invisible wall. My job is to penetrate that wall. I need to be relaxed and unhurried so that I can help him feel the same way. I'm not happy until I've created a sense of peace for me and the people around me." As McCarthy looks for a way to "engage, then disarm," the customer, body language becomes very important. "I establish eye contact to let him know that I am aware of his presence." Like other associates,

McCarthy welcomes the customer as if he were a guest in his home with comments such as: "How are you doing today? You look like you have a question."

■ The Selling Process

If the customer says he's looking for a navy blue suit, for example, McCarthy will escort him over to where that merchandise is displayed. Fit and color are his first considerations. He will venture an educated guess on the customer's size to "establish that I'm an experienced professional who knows his business. Then I'll suggest we try on a coat to make sure we have the right size. By doing that, we begin to bond." Bonding is essential. Because McCarthy is six-foot-six inches tall, he takes special care to identify with the customer. If a customer, who happens to be shorter in stature than average, jokes, "I bet you don't have too many suits in *my* size," McCarthy will counter with the flip side of the dilemma: "I bet we have fewer suits in *my* size than in yours." In essence, McCarthy is telling the customer that "he's not an oddball. In fact, I may be odder than he is. But the important thing is that we have established a connection." Throughout the process, McCarthy casually interviews the customer because the "more information you have, the better you can work. What kind of business is he in? What kind of clothes does he wear for business?" After showing him a selection of suits, McCarthy suggests the customer browse on his own for a minute or two. "It's like pheasant hunting. I don't want the dog to flush the bird too quickly. I want to let the customer settle down and then move around the department with some freedom. When he's ready, I'll be there to catch him." It's imperative to keep the process simple and easy by helping the customer eliminate the things he doesn't want and reducing the number of options down to two or three. "You cause confusion when you keep throwing things in and throwing things out until the customer is overloaded. Let's not make this brain surgery; this is simple stuff." McCarthy demonstrates his product knowledge by explaining the difference in fabrics, tailoring, and so on, and why particular colors or cuts or manufacturers are more flattering on one person than on another.

Price is never the primary issue for top Nordstrom sales performers. After determining the customer's size and tastes, Leslie Kaufman will ask for a ballpark price range. "I tell them, 'I don't want to show you a $1,200 suit and have you love it, and then find out that's not where we belong.' If you ask them first, most men will laugh at that; they're not embarrassed. I don't sell the highest priced suit if it doesn't fit the customer. If I find one is the best fit, then whatever else I pull out of the rack is going to be by that manufacturer."

McCarthy also doesn't like to talk about price. "The customer will tell me that as we go along," he said. "My responsibility is to make sure that the customer sees the best merchandise, so that's where we start. If a suit fits well, but it is out of his price range, I'll say, 'Let me show you the next best thing in terms of look.' But I explain why he isn't going to get as much at the lower price. I remind him that we all have stuff around the house that we wish we had never bought, and that we would have been happier if we had paid a little more for something that would last. If the suit fits, that's great. But, if he has a problem with the fit in the shoulder or with the collar, it won't look good and I won't feel good about selling it. I don't want him coming back in a month or two, saying he doesn't like it. I tell him that if, at some point, we could get him into the better-fitting suit, I would feel a lot better about it because I would feel that I was giving him the service he deserves.

"Throughout the process, I am constantly asking for his feedback on how the sleeves look and if the coat is cut the way he likes it," said McCarthy. "The more information I have, the better salesman I can be and the better I can serve the customer. I want to make sure that we are on the same page and that he has an investment in the decision-making process. This isn't just my deal. It's not an 'I' experience; it's a 'we' experience. With some customers, I need to plant the idea in his mind and let him think it over. Two weeks or a month later, he'll come back as if it was his idea." Leslie Kaufman heartily agreed with that approach: "I learned from my father that you never let the customer think *you* made the decision; let him think he's the one who decided to buy that extra suit. Give him some of that power; he came in to spend the money."

Often, customers have their own "picture" of what they want. But when the look that they want is not right for them, then it's up to the associate to change the picture. "A gentleman will come into my department, show me a newspaper advertisement for an Armani suit, and say, 'This is what I want to look like,'" said Kaufman. "But if he's round-shouldered and won't look good in Armani, I must be very diplomatic when I explain why this particular cut will not do him justice. If he insists, I'll let him try it on. I don't generally do that because it's important to not let a man see himself in a garment that doesn't fit— unless it's to prove a point."

After a customer buys a suit, McCarthy will review with him what tailoring needs to be done and when the suit will be ready to be picked up. "Part of our tacit contract is that I listen. By showing him that we're on the same page, we are solidifying our relationship."

At Nordstrom, with its commission-oriented culture, the ability to consistently sell a customer more than one item—i.e., multiple sales—is what is what distinguishes the top sales performers. Pacesetters like McCarthy and Kaufman are keenly aware that the sale is never over. McCarthy always asks the customer if there is anything else he needs while he is in the store. "Based on what he tells me, I might suggest shirts, ties, underwear, belts, or socks," said McCarthy. But during this entire process, regardless of how long it takes, "I never think about the cash register; it'll always be there."

On the footwear side, "The hardest thing to do is to sell the first pair of shoes," said David Butler, the Tacoma sales associate, "but once you sell the first pair, it's really easy." Butler likes to show the customer at least three different types of styles "including something new that she might like, but she hasn't thought of. I might mention to the customer that we've just gotten in a couple of new pairs that are similar to the shoes she's wearing. That approach opens up new possibilities and opportunities."

When associates put out the extra effort to "treat people like they're the most important thing in the world, they will come back to you," remarked Deborah Kirsch, who sells shoes at the Oak Brook Mall store. "I get many personal customers by investing the extra time." People who are difficult to fit are especially appreciative of the attention. "If a customer has one foot that's larger than the other, we'll take care of her. (Nordstrom is one of the few retailers that sells "mismated" pairs of shoes.) She'll tell her friends about the positive experience she had at Nordstrom. Many new people come into the department asking for me to wait on them because I helped their friend or their mother." Often, a busy customer on her way to do other shopping will stop by Kirsch's department (Brass Plum Shoes) just long enough to tell Kirsch the size, style, and color of the shoe she's looking for. Kirsch will then ring up the purchase on the customer's credit card number, put the package on hold or check it at the concierge desk for the customer to pick up on her way out the door.

■ Follow Through

Top associates don't look for the one spectacular sale that will make their day. Instead, they are committed to planting the seed for an ongoing business relationship and doing what's necessary to nurture that seed. Patrice Nagasawa's final question to the customer is always "What were you looking for that you didn't find?" Nagasawa then notes the request in her personal book and follows up with a phone call when she locates the item.

Joe Dover finds he "hooks" the customer when he calls him back a few days later to ask how the shoes are working out. "Ninety percent of the time, they're so stunned that you called, they remember you," Dover attested. Dover often invites a customer to come into the store to get his shoes shined, compliments of Joe Dover. "It's one of those fun little things that Nordstrom gives us the freedom to do. It costs me $1.25, but it's part of the cost of doing business. It gets them in the store. When they're ready for more shoes, they'll come and see me." (Nordstrom reimburses Dover for the cost of these shoe shines.)

On one of Van Mensah's follow-up calls, a surprised client told Mensah, "It's amazing that you called because I was just thinking about you." The customer needed to obtain matching blazers and white slacks for all the men in his son's upcoming wedding party in Florida. The customer told Mensah, "I don't know how to pull this off. Please take care of everything." One simple phone call generated Mensah almost $10,000 in sales.

At the end of the day, many associates write their thank-you notes. Leslie Kaufman always sends a brief letter, "even if it's the tenth time I've waited on that customer. I don't thank him for his *business,* but I thank him for his *loyalty* and tell him them that it's a pleasure to always be of service to him." Annette Armony writes her thank-you notes at her home in Portland, late in the evening while watching television; Deborah Kirsch mails hers on her way out of the Oak Brook Mall store, so "I can start the day with a clean slate," she said.

McCarthy echoed that philosophy: "I hate to start up first thing in the morning, so I like to make sure that there is nothing left to be done at the end of the day. Whatever isn't done is the first item on my list for the next day. Before I go on vacation, I set it up so that I'm busy the first week I return. It's like I never left."

KEYS TO SUCCESS

At Nordstrom, the priority is on selling, and the key to successful selling is providing outstanding customer service. Nordstrom wants to sell everybody. Through practice, experience, and commitment, Nordstrom's best associates have learned how not to lose a sale because they couldn't satisfy the customer.

- If you treat customers like royalty and let them know that you will take care of them, they usually come back to you.

- Nordstrom's top salespeople don't put things off until the end of the day. They get them out of the way so they can start the next day fresh.

- When customers enter a department, salespeople always make sure they are acknowledged. They are relaxed and unhurried in order to help the customer feel the same way.

- Top salespeople keep the process simple and easy by helping the customer eliminate the things he doesn't want. They constantly ask for feedback because the more information they have, the better they can serve the customer. Price is never a primary issue.

- "Trust" is the coin of the realm. Salespeople earn the confidence of customers by being well versed in the merchandise they sell. They aren't just selling clothes and shoes, they are also selling service.

- Top salespeople rely on the tools that Nordstrom provides, including a personal customer book to keep track of pertinent information on every customer.

- Multiple sales distinguish the top sales performers.

- The telephone is a powerful tool for generating business, improving productivity and saving time.

- Follow-through is important. Top salespeople aren't looking for the big score. They are committed to nurturing an ongoing business relationship.

Customer Service the Nordstrom Way

The Future

Retail has always been a fickle business; never more so than it is today, when customer loyalty is hard-earned and harder to maintain. The landscape and psychology of the industry have been transformed by a wide variety of factors: more choices of where to shop; changing buying habits; an aging population that is more interested in function than fashion; more working women; greater ethnic diversity; and an uncertain economic future. Today's busy consumers want retailers to save them time by providing them with convenience, reliability, efficiency, and, most importantly, merchandise that represents an obviously good value for the price.

"Retailing is a mature industry," said retail consultant Howard Davidowitz in *WWD*. "In a mature industry the consumer becomes the boss. They will tolerate nothing but excellence—there will be choices everywhere."

In this era of changing buying habits, consumers who want high quality and service at low prices are comfortable getting their shopping done in several different retail formats: traditional department stores (Macy's, Marshall Field, et al.); specialty stores (from the boutique on the

203

corner to The Gap); designer stores (Polo/Ralph Lauren, Laura Ashley); discounters (Wal-Mart, Kmart); off-price stores offering surplus, unsold or discontinued merchandise (Mervyn's, Marshall's); cavernous, no-frills warehouse membership "clubs" (PriceCostco, Sam's Club) that offer a small selection of in-season merchandise purchased directly from the manufacturer or indirectly from third parties; and manufacturer-owned factory outlet stores, which sell end-of-season and surplus merchandise.

Discounters and full-line retailers used to be segregated into different mall formats; today they operate virtually next door to each other in an increasing number of prime malls, where traditional department store anchors are being replaced by "category killers," such as Toys 'R' Us, and discounters for one simple reason: they draw shoppers. Today, discounters account for more than 40 percent of the general merchandise and more than 30 percent of apparel (particularly women's and children's) sold in this country. By the end of the century, "the categorization of retailing will disappear," predicted David A. Cole, chairman of the retailing consultant firm of Kurt Salmon Associates, in *Women's Wear Daily*. Cole believes that as pricing and merchandising formats blur, it will be impossible to strictly define retailers as discounters, department stores, or mass merchants. This reshuffling of the retail deck is not limited to suburban malls. For example, in the heart of downtown Philadelphia, a discount clothier called Daffy's owns and occupies the building that once housed the exclusive Bonwit Teller store.

The retail industry hobbled out of the 1980s with too many stores and too many shopping centers. From 1972 to 1991, retail space in the country's shopping centers and strip malls more than doubled from 7.9 square feet per person to 18.1 square feet, according to *Women's Wear*

Daily, as expansion-hungry retailers—lured by low-cost building and leasing arrangements—seized greater market share. But the game changed in the late eighties and early nineties with a wholesale weeding out of many unneeded retailers, including well-known department stores and upscale specialty stores. The survivors have been able to trade on their size, wide variety of merchandise, buying power, name familiarity, convenient locations, and proprietary credit cards. Some analysts predict that by the year 2000, there will be only a few national and regional department stores companies left—most likely Federated Department Stores (which swallowed up Macy's), Dillard Department Stores, and May Company Stores. As their profit margins grow slimmer because of increased competition, department stores must enhance operating efficiencies by spreading costs over more stores and using their buying clout to get better prices for merchandise.

■ The Nordstrom Response

How does this scenario affect customer service the Nordstrom way?

"It's our job to give good service in nice surroundings but not charge more than somebody who's selling out of a concrete box. We work hard at making sure we're not undersold," said Bruce Nordstrom. "As long as we're not being undersold on the fashionable items, then we can correctly say to the customer that we have the lowest price [on a particular item]; probably the only price, because [in many cases] the competition hasn't even gotten that item yet. We also have to be concerned about basic items [underwear, socks, etc.] because another store could sell them on a skinnier margin." Nordstrom also works at maintaining its regular prices. There are only two major sales a year, and the store marks down clothes to increase sales volume only as a last resort.

"Price/value" relationship has become a retailing buzzword for the nineties, an era when customers' allegiance to a particular store is strongly influenced by their belief that the price they are paying for an item is fair for the value received. Interestingly, although Nordstrom has stressed value in its advertising for many years, scores of faithful customers have written letters to the store to say that they don't want Nordstrom to over-emphasize its prices. "Customers tell us that if they were shopping solely on the basis of price, they would shop at a discounter," said Cynthia Paur, corporate merchandise manager for ready-to-wear, who was previously director of sales promotion. These customers say that they shop at Nordstrom for the service, selection, and the cachet that a Nordstrom gift box conveys. That attitude "has been interesting for us because when the economy was down [in the early 1990s], we emphasized pricing more than we ever had in the past. Now we've balanced it back. I think we should be known for great value, but I don't think our customers will ever allow us to be famous for low prices. They don't want that to be our prominent image."

One of the ways Nordstrom (like other major retailers) tries to maintain its prices—and still make a profit—is through private label merchandise, which is available in almost every category of goods that Nordstrom carries. Private label goods account for about 20 percent of Nordstrom's merchandise. It represents a small component of some departments and the foundation of others, such as dress shirts for men, which are about 90 percent private label. According to Bruce Nordstrom, "The success we have had with our dress shirt program, which led the way for our private label business, has told us that we should give the customer a better value than a brand name or designer shirt." With that strategy, "the private label will take on a life of its own; the customer will ask for it," added Bruce. "Ten years from now, today's hot designer may not be around, but Nordstrom will be. So we tell our people to be protective of our name." Jim Nordstrom summed up Nordstrom's private label products in four words: "value, quality, exclusivity, and size." For example, a pump shoe with the model name Sensation comes in sizes 3 to 13, from AAAA to E; the J.W. Nordstrom men's dress shirt, named after the store's founder, is available in sixty-one different sizes.

Bruce Nordstrom felt that many department stores prostitute their private label goods by manipulating them as a way to enhance gross margins, rather than provide quality. Private label goods "are the first things that go on sale; they're the weekend specials and sidewalk-sale merchandise. Stores can football items (lower and raise their price from day to day) because they bring the merchandise in at an inflated initial price. That's one of the principal reasons why better retailing is in such disarray right now." Nordstrom takes a different approach: "We're trying to offer a reasonable value all the time. We believe in getting a normal mark-on or even a less mark-on. You improve your gross margin by not having to meet the price of everybody all over town. We want to have everyday low prices. The customers are smart. They know what's going on."

According to a report conducted for *Women's Wear Daily*, discounters earned high marks for prices and bargains, but low marks for product quality and availability of familiar labels. Because their profit margins are so thin, discounters generally offer less service than conventional stores, but, confronted with increasing competition, they must find merchandising tools other than price to differentiate themselves. Many are elevating the quality and fashion of the product (which will improve profit margins), upgrading their window displays (and changing them more frequently), and, like Nordstrom, making their interiors more comfortable and inviting. They are even putting a greater emphasis on customer service, because no matter where people shop, they expect to be treated well. "A lot of people have made a giant leap to the conclusion that warehouse stores and discount stores are going to be the only stores left. I can't make that leap," said Bruce Nordstrom. He also questions whether warehouse and discount stores will continue to be a threat to Nordstrom in brand-name apparel, which is harder to discount than hard goods such as television sets. "Clothing is like bananas; it spoils real easy, and you've got to be real quick. That isn't their game; that's our game."

Nevertheless, Nordstrom does not intend to concede ground to the discounters; in fact, the company has quietly been a discounting pioneer with its Nordstrom Racks—small, self-service, high-tech, and low-overhead stores that dispose of end-of-season clearance merchandise that didn't sell in regular Nordstrom stores. Those goods are supplemented by special purchases from vendors Nordstrom usually does business with. Some lines are exclusive to the Rack and are not carried in regular Nordstrom stores. Nordstrom opened the first Rack in 1975 in the basement of the downtown Seattle flagship store as an outlet for the other floors. (Clearance shoes were displayed on fixtures called *racks*—hence the name.) By 1989, the concept was so successful it became a separate division with its own logo. As of 1995, there are nineteen Rack stores across the country. Nordstrom prefers to open one Rack for every three or four regular stores, in order to make it convenient to transport the goods for clearance. Racks (which range in size from 25,000 to 30,000 square feet) fulfill several purposes for Nordstrom: They introduce Nordstrom to customers who might be intimidated by the regular stores and they offer frequent Nordstrom shoppers another opportunity to buy Nordstrom goods. (Forty to 60 percent of Rack customers also shop at regular Nordstrom stores.) Corporately, the Racks (which employ more than 1,400 people), provide entry-level training and promotional opportunity for new employees, and generate more than 10 percent of total corporate profits.

Nordstrom has been experimenting with another discount concept called Last Chance Bargain Shoes and Apparel store, a 26,000 square foot unit, which is located in West Phoenix, Arizona. The store sells brands such as Nike, Guess, Reebok, Cole-Hahn, and Bostonian that haven't sold in the Nordstrom Rack; refurbished shoes; "as is" (shop-worn or damaged) items; and some new merchandise.

In 1993, Nordstrom briefly tested a 40,000 square foot, upscale outlet store, which was aimed at bargain-hunting affluent shoppers. Called Nordstrom Factory Direct (NFD), it opened in suburban Philadelphia's Franklin Mills mall, which also included outlets from Macy's, Sears, Saks Fifth Avenue, Spiegel, and J.C. Penney. NFD sold specially purchased end-of-season, off-season, and over-runs of first-quality men's and women's apparel, footwear, and accessories from such brand-name and designer labels as Jones New York, Esprit, Anne Klein II, Bill Blass, Chaps by Ralph Lauren, Levi's and Nike—as well as Nordstrom private label merchandise—at discounts of 20 to 70 percent. But after six months, Nordstrom converted it to a Rack because the supply from vendors was uneven and customers were disappointed with the merchandise; they had expected to find goods that were carried in the full-line Nordstrom stores. "We think that the NFD concept probably is valid, but it's going to take a long time to develop it," John Nordstrom told shareholders at the annual meeting in May 1994. "Right now our Racks are doing very well and we just thought this was a good time to change the NFD into a proven winner."

■ Shopping at Home

Many retailers and wholesalers are exploring other avenues for driving their business because, in many cases, sales growth through regular stores is barely outpacing the rate of inflation. In addition, crime and the perception of crime is changing shopping habits. Many consumers are reducing their evening shopping, carrying less cash, and spending fewer hours in malls. As a result, they are shopping at home through traditional mail order catalogs, home-shopping television networks, television infomercials, computer E-mail, the Internet, and, soon, by interactive television. Forty percent of U.S. households were expected to experiment with electronic shopping via TV or computer by the end of 1995, according to a poll by Yankelovich Partners published in *USA Today* in June 1994. David A. Cole of Kurt Salmon Associates predicted in *Women's Wear Daily* that by the year 2001, non-store retailing (including catalog and TV shopping) will account for 55 percent of general merchandise, apparel, and furniture sales, up from 15 percent in 1992.

Home shopping has become a $2.5 billion-a-year business. The two major cable TV shopping channels—QVC (which has a special lifestyle channel called Q2 that caters to affluent shoppers interested in health, fitness, and home decorating) and the Home Shopping Network (HSN)—each control about 49 percent of the home shopping market, and have a combined audience reach of almost 100 million cable viewers and satellite dish owners. In 1993, QVC received its first infusion of upscale credibility when Saks Fifth Avenue sold close to $600,000 worth of its Real Clothes in-house brand of casual, moderately priced sportswear. QVC also offers apparel from such well known designers as Diane Von Furstenberg, Arnold Scaasi, Bob Mackie, and Kenneth Jay Lane. Similar ventures between TV shopping channels and traditional retailers are inevitable. In 1994, R.H. Macy & Company, the New York retailing giant, announced plans to launch TV Macy's, a twenty-four-hour-a-day, seven-day-a-week national shopping channel, under the direction of creative consultant Don Hewitt, the long-time executive producer of CBS's *60 Minutes.* Home Shopping Network, which is an equity partner in TV Macy's, was slated to fill the orders, warehouse and distribute the goods, and provide customer service. As of this writing, TV Macy's was put on hold, awaiting the finalization of Federated Stores' acquisition of Macy's.

In 1994, Spiegel, the giant mail order company, and Time Warner Entertainment launched two new home shopping channels on cable television to sell merchandise for the family and the home. The first, called " Catalog 1," is a "video mall" service offering fashion accessories, children's products, and home furnishings from several different catalog companies, including Spiegel, Spiegel's Eddie Bauer division, Neiman-Marcus, Crate & Barrel, Williams-Sonoma, The Sharper Image, The Nature Company, and Time Warner's Viewer's Edge. The second channel, tested on Time Warner's cable system in Orlando, Florida, is fully interactive, enabling consumers to use a special remote control device to "enter" any catalog store at any time, view merchandise in full-motion video, and make purchases. Even MTV is experimenting with its own home shopping channel.

Some analysts believe QVC could be the biggest retailer in the country in twenty-five years and that television shopping could be the ruin of conventional retailers. But other industry watchers are less sanguine. One of their arguments is that not all cable subscribers are actually watching shopping channels; another argument is that the majority of home shoppers are people with too much free time and too little interest in high-end merchandise. (Perhaps that explains why inexpensive jewelry accounts for 44 percent of home shopping sales.) Then there are the return rates. According to *Women's Wear Daily,* home shopping return rates are comparable to those of mail order catalogs—from 15 percent for jewelry to 70 percent for high-priced holiday dresses. QVC claims that 18 percent of overall merchandise and 25 percent of apparel is returned; HSN claims that 20 percent of overall merchandise is returned, compared with 18.5 percent of apparel purchases. "Returns run the costs way up and increase markdowns," said John Nordstrom. "Merchandise is out floating around for months before they get it back, and by then it's worth nothing."

Shopping via television is certainly more convenient than in-store shopping, but it lacks the immediate sensual gratification. "Part of the reason you go to a retail store is to people watch," said John Nordstrom. "That's more important than people realize. We have a customer in downtown San Francisco who comes in every three months, just like clockwork, and buys six Hickey-Freeman suits. We preorder the suits and have them there for him when he comes into the store. He doesn't want them sent to his home because he wants to stand in front of the mirror and have his wife look at him. He likes the experience."

Still, Nordstrom is experimenting with home shopping as a way to expand its sales base by providing customers with more options to buy Nordstrom products and to capitalize on its enhanced national name recognition. In June 1993, Nordstrom joined with Bloomingdale's in a closed-circuit home shopping show, originating from the Bloomington, Minnesota, Mall of America, where both retailers are anchor stores. Unlike QVC or HSN, which sell their merchandise from television studios, the one-hour Mall of America show (produced by the National Broadcasting Company's NBC Direct subsidiary) was staged in the actual stores. Using a toll-free telephone number, viewers could order from Nordstrom a hopsack blazer in four colors, priced at $88; a $40 silk shell; $36 stirrup pants; and a "wallet on a strap" at $48. The wallet was the best seller. Nordstrom was underwhelmed by the results of its initial experience.

John Nordstrom doubted that there are enough consumers "sitting in front of their TV set, waiting for something to come up that they want to buy. Time is too valuable for people to do that. I think they want to push a button, see what they want to see, order it, and get on their way."

■ Direct Sales Division

With that reasoning, Nordstrom is committed to exploring other in-home shopping alternatives. The first of those options is a Direct Sales Division, launched in 1993 under the direction of general manager Daniel Nordstrom, son of Jim Nordstrom. The division is taking a two-pronged approach. The first stage, which began in spring 1994, was a series of catalogs that were mailed to 750,000 households across the country, particularly in areas where there were currently no nearby Nordstrom stores. (Nordstrom has long sent out catalogs, including a successful series featuring only private label merchandise, but the company considered them essentially an advertising vehicle for the goods in the stores.) The Direct Sales division is self-sustaining; it buys, produces, and is responsible for its own inventory and its own profit and loss. The company wants to see whether home shopping works best via a dedicated catalog division or through the stores themselves. Because it's a brand new business, "We need to understand the kinds of items that sell [through direct mail catalogs] and how to service the customer," said Bruce Nordstrom. "I'm pretty confident we'll be able to do that." Although the catalog division was not profitable in its first year, the company expects it to be profitable soon.

Although many of the services can be found from other catalogs, Nordstrom separates itself from the competition in several ways that emphasize customer service. Toll-free phone orders are handled from Seattle by "personal shoppers," not order-taking operators. (Unlike in-store Nordstrom sales people, these personal shoppers do not work on commission.) Shipping is dispensed from a new catalog distribution center in Memphis, Tennessee, near the national headquarters of Federal Express, in order to make it easier to facilitate orders. Nordstrom offers free Federal Express pick-up of merchandise that customers want to return. To make it easier to send items back, a return label is included with all merchandise. A special toll-free TDD telephone number is available for customers who are hearing impaired.

Interactive television, which offers a broad product selection targeted for upscale viewers, is the other facet of Nordstrom's home shopping strategy. Interactive television, which is in its nascent stage, is expected to be a more convenient, intimate, and immediate approach that enables the customer to communicate directly with an on-screen Nordstrom salesperson ("personal shopper") through a voice-activated conferencing system, which is two-way audio/one-way video, so that the personal shopper doesn't invade the privacy of the customer. The customer, who addresses the TV screen to trigger options, can examine the merchandise from several angles and can ask the personal shopper (seen in an on-screen window insert) questions about size, color, and so on. Once the customer makes her decision, she uses an on-screen menu to select method of payment and shipment.

Nordstrom believes personalized interactive shopping is better suited to the Nordstrom brand of customer service because its personal shoppers can directly assist customers. The format also encourages multiple sales because the customer can request to view any kind of merchandise. As an additional service, customers will be able to access prerecorded tapes for helpful information, such as how to tie a bow tie.

Interactive television shopping is only a few years away; it will take that long for homes throughout the United States to be wired for the system, which will be part of the "information superhighway" of digital and fiber optic technologies that will transform the way Americans shop, bank, learn, and communicate. Nordstrom has been exploring partnerships with technology companies, other retailers, and catalog companies in a future video shopping mall. In autumn 1994, Nordstrom began teaming up with U.S. West, the regional telephone company, to test selling merchandise in the Midwest via interactive television. The U.S. West interactive video merchandise service is offered in a variety of technologies, including television and personal computers. Nordstrom, J.C. Penney, and Land's End are also working on a similar system with Bell Atlantic, the East coast telephone company. U.S. West and

Nordstrom seem to have been on the same wavelength for a while. The same day that Nordstrom unveiled its plans for interactive shopping (at the 1993 annual shareholders meeting), U.S. West and Time Warner announced their own intentions to combine telephone and cable technologies to provide instant-order shopping, movies on demand, video games, and other entertainment and information services. Some analysts predict that interactive shopping has the potential to become a $100 billion-plus business in 10 years.

In October 1994, Nordstrom launched its own E-mail shopping service called Nordstrom Personal Touch America (NPTA), a collaboration with long-distance phone carrier MCI Communications Corporation and ConnectSoft, a software communications company. Every request or order to NPTA is answered in the downtown Seattle flagship store by a Nordstrom personal shopper, who is expected to give the same kind of customer service that Pat McCarthy and his colleagues give, such as matching up the customer with the right merchandise, keeping records of the customer's sizes, preferred styles, wedding anniversary date, and so on. "Anyone out there in the E-mail world can communicate with a live person," said Pat Adkisson, operations and business manager for Nordstrom's direct sales division, in *Women's Wear Daily.* "It's a way to do suggestive selling." For personal computer and modem users not currently linked to any E-mail service, Nordstrom offers a special software package called Nordstrom Connection, which enables the shopper to connect with Nordstrom via Prodigy, CompuServe, and MCI Mail.

Nordstrom is also exploring other technology options, including a future system that will enable airline passengers to order goods from computers attached to the back of the seat in front of them. Other companies are offering interactive shopping systems via personal computers that read CD-ROM disks, which serve as electronic catalogs for one merchant, or display many items in a specific catalog from a wide variety of merchants. Using this technology, with the touch of a mouse, the shopper is able to see how a particular shirt looks in every color available. Whatever system Nordstrom ultimately uses, the personal touch of customer service has to be a part of it.

■ Forging Strong Vendor Partnerships

In another strategy to differentiate itself from the competition, Nordstrom has been working on exclusive marketing alliances and relationships with a wide assortment of vendors (who want to reach their target customers through a reliable retailer). Since 1989, Nordstrom has been the exclusive U.S. licensee for Faconnable (pronounced fa-so-NA-bleh), a Nice-based men's apparel line that is carried in Faconnable stores throughout France, Western Europe, and Japan. Nordstrom carries Faconnable tailored clothing, sportswear, furnishings, and accessories in more than fifty of its stores. In October 1993, Nordstrom, in partnership with Faconnable, opened the first free-standing Faconnable store on Fifth Avenue at 54th Street in New York—Nordstrom's first foray into the Manhattan retail jungle. Nordstrom, which oversaw the physical renovation of the building and opening of the 5,200-square-foot store, manages the day-to-day operations and hires and trains the sales force. For the 1994 Olympic Games, the male CBS-TV announcers and reporters wore Faconnable clothes in exchange for on-air mentions. The women announcers were outfitted in Classiques, a Nordstrom private-label line.

Similar to its Faconnable agreement, Nordstrom signed an exclusive licensing agreement in 1994 with Hickey-Freeman to source and distribute a line of dress shirts, neckwear, formal vests, and cummerbund and bow ties sets under the Hickey-Freeman label. The line debuted for Father's Day 1994. The arrangement is for three years, after which the collection will be offered to other top retailers.

Nordstrom hopes its new direct mail division will be an opportunity to develop the Faconnable and Classiques label, other Nordstrom private labels, as well as a new line of women's and men's golf-oriented sportswear and footwear under the Callaway Golf Company label. In 1993, Nordstrom entered into an exclusive licensing agreement with Callaway (most famous for its "Big Bertha" drivers and irons) to develop, design, and manufacture the line and sell it in Nordstrom stores throughout the United States, which began in spring 1994. Callaway, which is based in Carlsbad, California, receives a 5 percent royalty on sales. The agreement was considered the first time a well-known retailer and an equipment manufacturer have teamed up for an apparel license.

Beginning in 1992, Nordstrom has given its Nordstrom Partners in Excellence Award to vendors "whose products and business practices best exemplify our commitments to quality and value, service and integrity." Nordstrom wanted to find a way "to recognize the people who do it the best; people who not only make the best products but are honest and ethical and really a pleasure to be partners with; people who care about our success and people whose success we care about," said Bruce Nordstrom. Past winners include the Estee Lauder Companies, the Hickey-Freeman Company, and the Dexter Shoe Company.

In 1994, Nordstrom introduced "The Nordstrom Partnership," a set of worldwide business guidelines for use with its vendors, because, according to Gail Cottle, executive vice-president of women's product development, "With the increased amount of sourcing [production] we are doing throughout the world and the growth of our business, we wanted to make clear our stands of conduct for our business partners."

The guidelines are as follows:

1. **Legal Requirements:** Nordstrom expects all of its partners to comply with applicable laws and regulations of the United States and those of the respective country of manufacture or exportation. All products must be accurately labeled and clearly identified as to their country of origin.

2. **Health and Safety Requirements:** Nordstrom seeks partners who provide safe and healthy work environments for their workers, including adequate facilities and protections from exposure to hazardous conditions or materials.

3. **Employment Practices:** Nordstrom firmly believes people are entitled to equal opportunity in employment. Although the company recognizes cultural differences exist, Nordstrom pursues business partners who do not discriminate and who demonstrate respect for the dignity of all people.

4. **Environmental Standards:** Partners must demonstrate a regard for the environment, as well as compliance with local environmental laws. Further, Nordstrom seeks partners who demonstrate a commitment to progressive environmental practices and to preserving the earth's resources.

5. Documentation and Inspection: Nordstrom intends to monitor compliance with our Partnership Guidelines and to undertake on-site inspection of partners facilities. Nordstrom will review and may terminate its relationship with any partner found to be in violation of the Partnership Guidelines.

Nordstrom's social consciousness was recognized in the 1994 edition of *Shopping for a Better World,* a guidebook published by Sierra Club Books, joining companies such as Ben & Jerry's, Tom's of Maine, and General Mills.

■ Improving the Bottom Line

After years of meteoric growth in the 1970s and 1980s, Nordstrom's corporate earnings, like the earnings of many retailers (with the rare exception of Wal-Mart on one end of the fashion spectrum and The Gap on the other) flattened out in the first few years of the 1990s. In 1992, sales were $3.42 billion, a 7.6 percent increase over 1991's $3.18 billion. But earnings increased only 0.6 percent, from $136.6. million in 1992, compared with $135.8 million the previous year. One major reason was the near-depression in California (where half of Nordstrom's stores are located), which for several years had gone through its worst financial decline since the end of World War II. Nordstrom was forced "to live with California in the nineties like we prospered with them in the eighties," said co-chairman Jack McMillan. "It was fun in the eighties, and it [was] not so much fun in the nineties." The game had changed and Nordstrom had to adjust.

Jammie Baugh, executive vice-president and general manager of Nordstrom's southern California region, said, "We had to figure out a way to keep our standards up, reach for everything we could possibly get, and, at the same time, keep morale up and keep people happy. That was a real challenge. We had to focus on the things that we have control over. The one thing that we have absolute control over is the experience our customers have in the store. So, we worked on that. We had a unique opportunity because in the eighties, when everybody was doing well, our competitors began to focus more on service because they could afford to do it. But the minute it got tough, that's the first place they cut. Frankly, although we did well in the eighties, I think we lost some of our margin ahead of the competition in regard to service. The tough economic times presented us with an opportunity to widen the gap, again, if we were good enough to do that. I think we've done that. Our people have risen to the occasion."

Thanks to improved business in California (where Nordstrom has almost half of its sales space) and other parts of the country, better buying trends, and fewer markdowns on merchandise Nordstrom's financial performance began turning around in the middle of 1993. By the end of that year, corporate earnings had advanced 2.8 percent to $140.4 million or $1.71 a share, from $136.6 million or $1.67 a share, and sales gained 4.9 percent to $3.59 billion from $3.4 billion. The performance was even better in 1994. For the year, net earnings increased 44.5 percent to $202.9 million, or $2.47 per share, and sales increased 8.5 percent to $3.89 billion. These figures were brought about by better buying (thus fewer markdowns); tighter controls over expenses (thanks to a new inventory-management system); an upswing in the sales of women's apparel; sales gains of 4.4 percent in stores opened one year or more; better-than-expected results from its Direct Sales catalog division; expansion and remodeling of some older stores; and the successful opening of new stores in Annapolis, Maryland;

Santa Anita, California; Portland, Oregon; and Skokie, Illinois. Nordstrom also returned to the good graces of Wall Street. The price of its stock, which had been mired in the mid-$20 range, climbed back up to the mid-$40 range by the end of 1994. (These were the last available financial figures before this book was published.)

Because Nordstrom doesn't foresee immediate significant profit increases through greater sales alone, the company (like every retailer) is dealing with rising costs on a variety of fronts and is constantly looking for places to cut expenses, such as the buying, delivery, and selling of the merchandise. At a time when other big retailers were operating state-of-the-art merchandising systems and inventory and expense controls, Nordstrom was, until 1993, reluctant to follow suit. Nordstrom felt that most retail computer systems were designed for centralized inventory and accounting purposes, which goes against its decentralized, individualized structure. In other words, the company didn't want computers replacing people. Because its decentralized system is so unique, "we couldn't use an off-the-shelf software package. We had to design our own," said Jim Nordstrom. In 1993, Nordstrom installed a multi-million dollar computerized system that links all of its stores and corporate headquarters; provides managers and buyers with product-by-product information to track inventory; analyzes sales activity; identifies customer buying trends; makes purchasing decisions; creates pricing strategies; and monitors the performance of suppliers. The system also helped reduce markdowns, facilitated more timely re-ordering, and lowered labor costs. (The only thing the old system did was record sales.) Nordstrom installed computer terminals near the cash registers, which enables salespeople to keep track of all the items in their department and to find other stores that have an item that a customer has requested. The computer also keeps track of other information, such as the ten best- and ten worst-selling items in a department. As exact as the new system is, Nordstrom does not want to radically change its culture by becoming, like so many other big retailers, over-reliant on computer read-outs. "What makes us unique is buying from the gut," explained co-president John Whitacre. "We run our stores like old-fashioned merchants." Agreeing with Whitacre was Jennifer Black Groves, executive vice-president and retail analyst, Black and Company, a Portland, Oregon, brokerage firm, who approvingly told *Women's Wear Daily* that Nordstrom was "not letting the technology replace the personal touch. This is what is so key and so exciting."

Despite the rising costs of employees (particularly in health care benefits), the number of associates on the sales floor is "literally the last place you want to cut," said Bruce Nordstrom. "We want our floors stocked with motivated, enthusiastic, hard-working salespeople." At another kind of retail company, "an accountant would come in and say, 'You have twenty salespeople in a department; starting tomorrow, you're going to have fifteen salespeople.' It isn't that simple. This is a sensitive area; you can't just go in with a meat ax. When stores hang on to people but cut their hours, they end up with a cadre of part-time people who are no longer giving good service because they're not happy." Instead, Nordstrom is continuing to pare from its payrolls its lowest-producing sales people so that, ideally, more customers will be waited on by the top producers. "That will result in better customer service and higher sales, and more income for the superstars," said Bruce Nordstrom. "We want them to be happy."

■ Expansion

Because of its financial position, Nordstrom is one of the strongest players left in retailing and will be one of the survivors for the 1990s and beyond. The keenly competitive Nordstrom family, which has always considered growth a yardstick of success, continues to have an aggressive battle plan for store expansion, thanks to its strong cash flow and relatively low long-term debt, which makes the company attractive to the financial equity markets. Not surprisingly, mall developers give Nordstrom first call on the most desirable retail space and the most desirable terms on that space. Typically, powerhouse anchor stores such as Nordstrom, which serve as the main draws for the mall, are rewarded with low rents that are subsidized by the mall developers.

Nordstrom still has much of the United States to cover and has room to enlarge its presence in major markets where it already does business, such as the metropolitan New York and Chicago areas. The company is poised to grow after being thwarted during the first few years of the 1990s by a combination of developers' problems in securing financing and a series of obstacles set up by fearful competing retailers who filed frivolous lawsuits and environmental impact objections. In Portland, the May Department Stores Company challenged Nordstrom's plans to rebuild Nordstrom's Washington Square mall store, citing potential parking and traffic problems. Woodward & Lothrop impeded the construction of Nordstrom's store in Annapolis; and the May Company did the same thing in Denver. Nevertheless, by 1996 Nordstrom expects to add nine full-line stores, which will be located in Schaumburg, Illinois; Indianapolis, Indiana; Short Hills, New Jersey; White Plains, New York; Dallas, Texas;

Auburn, Washington; Troy, Michigan; King of Prussia, Pennsylvania; and Denver, Colorado.

Some people (even a few inside Nordstrom) think expansion should be slowed because, they believe, the company doesn't have enough top people. Nordstrom management disagrees. One reason Nordstrom continues to expand is to attract good people and keep them motivated with opportunities to ascend the corporate ladder. "With our decentralized system, each division has a life of its own," said Bruce Nordstrom. "If they are carrying out their missions and we feel good about the way they are developing, we will have ourselves new general managers and buyers as we go into new regions." (As we saw in Chapter 3, in new markets and old, these managers and buyers carry on the culture.)

Nordstrom also encourages experienced Pacesetters and Customer Service All-Stars to mentor new sales associates. "Being number one is not as important to me as it used to be," said David Butler, the top shoe salesman from Tacoma. "I'm getting older. [He's approaching fifty.] It would be very selfish of me not to share with other people what I have been able to accomplish. I am trying to help teach others what it takes to become a Pacesetter and give them the tools to do it. It's a lot more fun for me helping the entire department make their day, which helps the store make its day." Pat McCarthy tries to do the same thing. "I tell new associates to learn everything this company has to offer, keep the good, build on it, and discard the rest. If you decide to go into business for yourself, you can make that commitment knowing what it takes to be successful," said McCarthy.

Keeping good workers with the company is just as important as attracting new ones. Alice Dick, who sells couture clothing in Portland, is a perfect example. She joined

Nordstrom in 1969, at the age of fifty-one, which is a period she good-naturedly calls her "middle-essence." Although she had been working in retail since the age of nineteen (primarily with small specialty stores in Oregon), Alice became a Pacesetter for the first time at the age of seventy ("I guess maybe I wasn't as go-go-go before," she quipped.); she's been one for the past six years. She has no intention of retiring. "When Ronald Reagan became president, the Nordstroms eliminated their informal retirement age. They decided that if an employee is doing the job and is happy with it, and is able to hold up her end, they have no problem," said Alice. "They came up with an arrangement where I work my 1,000 hours a year."

■ The Challenge of Diversity

According to the U.S. Census Bureau, between 1992 and 2000, the percentage growth in the number of people of African, Hispanic, Asian, and Native American descent will surpass that of Caucasians. Consequently, over the past few years, Nordstrom has focused on how to respond to the ethnic diversity of its customers as well as its sales associates and suppliers. Diversity has been a corporate goal since 1987, when several minority employees in Seattle got the company's attention by filing discrimination complaints with the Equal Employment Opportunity Commission. Since then, Nordstrom has made a concerted effort to hire and promote people of color and to reach out to their communities. "We are committed to having a sales force that reflects the communities that we are in, and to have them represented in our advertising," said Jack McMillan. Today, nearly 30 percent of employees (including 19 percent of management) are people of color. More than one-third of the models Nordstrom uses in ads and catalogs are people of color.

In addition, Nordstrom created a Minority Business Development Program to cultivate minority-owned vendors of office supplies, food, music, photography, and other services. To get out the word, Nordstrom advertises in minority-owned publications and operates a toll-free phone line for information on opportunities for minorities. In 1993, Nordstrom spent more than $120 million with minority and/or women-owned vendors—compared with $500,000 in 1989. In 1992 and 1993, Nordstrom was selected to the Hispanic 100, a group of companies catering to that community. Every year since 1990, Nordstrom has sponsored the Nordstrom Community Service Awards, which recognizes the efforts of individuals who have made a difference in their communities. The awards are given at a banquet called "A Salute to Cultural Diversity," which raises money for inner-city schools and social service agencies. In 1994, the Seattle banquet's guest speaker and presenter was actor Edward James Olmos. In 1993, those duties were performed by actor Danny Glover. Nordstrom has held similar events in Los Angeles and Chicago.

Nordstrom has also been making itself more accessible to disabled customers—a large, relatively untapped market—by developing an employee sensitivity-training program and improving access in the stores, such as widening aisles for wheelchairs. In 1993, Nordstrom was the recipient of the first-ever Chairman's Award, given by the President's Committee on Employment of People with Disabilities. The company also received honors from the National Easter Seal Society and the Los Angeles County Commission on Disabilities. Since 1991, Nordstrom has been including fashion models with disabilities in its catalogs and other marketing campaigns. When the first catalog showing models in wheelchairs came out, "the letters came pouring in from businesses, schools, agencies, parents who have children with disabilities," recalled

Cynthia Paur, who at the time was executive vice-president of sales promotion. "We have never had more positive consumer response on any single thing we have ever done. It was a natural evolution of our model diversity. We've always tried to have our models look a little more natural than a typical model. Since 1968, we have used a range of races. We've been more conscientious as the years have gone by. We are saying to anyone of varying size, shape, race, or age, 'we want your business.'"

What can other businesses learn from the Nordstrom way? Betsy Sanders, the former Nordstrom executive who is now a director of Wal-Mart, said, "Nordstrom and Wal-Mart share the characteristics of building on what works. They don't say, 'We've been in this business for a hundred years and we know better.' They ask themselves: 'What are we doing now that we could be doing better?' They keep reworking it; they stumble and improve, stumble and improve. At their best, Wal-Mart and Nordstrom never lose the awareness that they don't have all the answers. They know that the customer has all the information that they need. They know that the salespeople—the ones who are closest to the customer—are truly the most valuable people in the company, so they each have a system that gives salespeople everything they need. And in return, the salespeople give their managers valuable intelligence on how to make the business successful."

A 1994 *Fortune* magazine article entitled "Finding, Training & Keeping The Best Service Workers" summed up what Nordstrom has always done and what American business is finally catching onto: "At a time when service counts more than ever, companies are rediscovering the importance of the people who actually deliver it. . . . Pressed to 'delight' their value-driven customers, companies are scrambling to hire, train, and hang on to ordinary mortals who can perform feats of extraordinary service." Today's successful service employees "are resilient and resourceful, empathetic and enterprising, competent and creative."

■ The Importance of Family

After all is said and done, Nordstrom's supreme advantage over its competition is that it has been—and will continue to be—controlled and operated by the Nordstrom family. "That takes 90 percent of the politics out of it," said Barden Erickson, the retired vice-president of store planning. "You don't have the backbiting and the bootlicking." The Nordstroms still exercise management by walking around. "It's so powerful when they come around to talk to our people and remind them that our company is only as good as they are—today and every day," said Len Kuntz, the corporate sales promotion director. Sales associate Leslie Kaufman describes the "feeling of joy" she gets when John Nordstrom visits the Westside store. "He never lets me forget how happy the Nordstrom family is that I'm with them," said Kaufman. "That feels good."

With the exception of Dillard Department Stores, Belk Store Services, and Strawbridge and Clothier, the great stores of America are no longer controlled or operated by the descendants of the clever merchants who created the business and knew what the customer wanted. It's not that professional managers can't brilliantly run the Macy's, Saks, and Neiman-Marcuses of the world; it's just that in a era when top retail executives change department stores as fast as free agents switch baseball teams, continuity is measured by quarterly earnings; not generations. The connection to the founder's original vision usually vanishes by the second generation, and is almost unheard of in the third. Nordstrom is already deep into the fourth generation, with no fewer than six sons (in their thirties) of John, Bruce, and James Nordstrom in management positions.

Family control brings with it an institutional memory, a consistent message and stability for long-range planning. "We run the business like our dads did," said Jim Nordstrom. "It's a different business, but our fundamentals are the same. It'll be the same next year and the year after and the year after. The goal doesn't get changed on our people." Sudden corporate changes "demotivate people."

Customer service consultant Peter Glen writes: "Companies that manage service the best are those that develop a policy and then stick to it. This is very difficult in an age of mergers, acquisitions, and brand-new management every week. It paralyzes middle managers and dumbfounds customers to find that whatever was true last week is not true now, and might change again after Friday. When this happens often enough, employees who work there tend to go into 'hold' and do nothing."

The Nordstrom family is not insulated from non-Nordstrom thinking. The board of directors includes several outside advisers with no vested interest in the company, and the management team is a mix of non-family and family members. In 1991, Nordstrom created a new level of management, four co-presidents (all in their forties), who took over the day-to-day responsibilities of the co-chairmen. This extra layer of bureaucracy triggered a negative reaction on Wall Street because it went against Nordstrom's reputation for lean management. It also proved to be unwieldy, and two years later two of the co-president positions were eliminated.

The remaining co-presidents, Raymond Johnson and John Whitacre, bridge the transition between generations of Nordstroms. In 1995, Bruce Nordstrom turned sixty-one; John Nordstrom fifty-eight, Jim Nordstrom fifty-five, and Jack McMillan sixty-three. None of them are working because they need the money. John compared his motivation at age fifty-eight to his father Elmer's motivation at the same age. "My dad told me if I didn't want to be in this business, he would leave tomorrow," John recalled. The fact that John's son James A., vice-president and general manager of the Northern California region "is as involved as he is and likes [the business] so much, is what keeps me going, and I'm sure it's the same way with Bruce and Jim." Bruce has three sons in the company: Blake W., vice-president and general manager of the Washington state region; Erik, Midwest regional manager and general manager of the Mall of America (Bloomington, Minnesota) store; and Peter, manager of the Orange Country region. Jim has two sons: William, corporate merchandise manager, accessories, and Daniel, general manager of the Direct Sales Division.

The fourth generation, despite being individually wealthy in their own right, are unusual in the fact that so many of them have joined the business and are willing to start at the bottom (along with everybody else) and work their way up. "They are motivated enough to go through the paces. That's our standard here, and there are no exceptions," said John Nordstrom, who did admit, however, "We have moved them ahead faster than we would move someone else ahead. . . . They've had to get their fingers burned along the way, just like we did."

Not surprisingly, the sheer number of up-and-coming Nordstrom family members have stirred some grumbling among a few managers, who complain that when a top job (such as store manager) opens up, instead of seeking the best person for the job, they are pressured to fill the post with a family member. They claim that each senior Nordstrom lobbies for his own offspring. Such criticism is not unusual in a family-controlled business. What sets Nordstrom apart is that there are so many Nordstroms. Consequently, the young Nordstroms' stiffest competition is with each other. Soon, that will need to be sorted out. There is no question that after the current senior generation retires, a combination of family and non-family members will run the company because the active presence and involvement of family members is the guarantee that Nordstrom will remain Nordstrom; without them, it would be a different company. "The Nordstroms have not been titular executives. They have been involved and instrumental in every aspect of the company," said Betsy Sanders. "It's critical for the fourth generation to continue that."

Succession is certainly a key issue. Directors have been bringing in all the members of the fourth generation one at a time "to talk to the board about what they are doing. So the board can get to know them as they mature and grow in the company," said director John F. Harrigan, retired chairman of Union Bank, Los Angeles. "That's a very important process that will have to continue for a little while. The company is bigger and a lot more complex to get your hands around. They are going to need a variety of experiences in the company."

Director Alfred E. Osborne, Jr., said, "it's a little early to tell how [the succession] is going to play out. I think there is a commitment from the next generation to be part of the tradition that has been established and I think they will rise to the occasion. I don't know which ones will shake out, but the ones that I've been exposed to are all very capable."

Osborne, who is director of the Entrepreneurial Studies Center and associate professor of business economics in The John E. Anderson Graduate School of Management of the University of California, Los Angeles, said that the next generation's most obvious challenge is achieving as much success as the previous generation, but in a much more difficult market. He is confident that the younger Nordstroms are aware of the challenges that they are going to face—such as new technologies and new forms of product distribution—and are "well grounded, well educated, and very capable" of dealing with those challenges. He envisions "the survival of the collaborative management approach that the Nordstroms have pioneered. This new group has grown up with it all their lives and they have the benefit of not knowing any better way to do it." To continue and maintain the management model that achieved the success of the past "is a very powerful motivator," added Osborne. "Now, whether that model can work in the business environment of the twenty-first century is an open question, but I think it has a good chance. The signals go to support the Nordstrom model—rather than a hierarchical model- -because the world is moving to greater participation, more shared decisions, more decisions at the point of service. Workers at all levels of the organization are empowered by both technology and information, all of which means more collaboration, all of which means shrinking hierarchies. Which means that the old-fashioned Nordstrom approach to management may be what the twenty-first century is all about and is what will be increasingly adopted by a variety of organizations."

A 1994 article in the *New York Times* entitled "Industry is Learning to Love Agility," indicated that there is a trend toward "agile" companies that are "able to switch quickly and economically from one product to another with very little disruption." These companies are also striving "to establish closer relationships with suppliers and customers in an effort to react more quickly to shifts in markets. . . . Unlike traditional manufacturers, with their hierarchical management and emphasis on sheer output, agile companies stress sharing of information and power across the organization, alliances with suppliers and customers, and fast responses to changing market conditions." This point was reaffirmed in another *Times* article, published around the same time, that claimed, ". . . people skills—almost universally called the 'soft stuff' of business—may be the key to survival, human resources is taking on new significance. Increasingly, its practitioners are being included in strategic decision making, sitting on the powerful committees, and reporting directly to the highest executive levels." All of these so-called "trends" certainly sound like the tenets of customer service the Nordstrom way.

Looking toward the future, Bruce Nordstrom and his fellow co-chairmen "feel good about the foundation, the work ethic, and the knowledge of the business that this [fourth] generation has. If there's a vision for the future, it's going to come from brains younger than ours, and that doesn't bother me in the least little bit; I encourage it. It worries me that when somebody comes up with an idea, my kneejerk reaction is, 'We tried that ten years ago and it didn't work.' I've seen it all. I don't want to be that way. Everything ought to get a careful consideration." For example, Nordstrom initially rejected the idea of establishing a separate direct mail catalog division several years ago because the same investment could be made in a store and it would come back a lot faster. "But today, more and more people want to shop at home, so we realized that we'd better start working on it."

The underlying Nordstrom culture and philosophy is not difficult to pass on to the next generation because it's simple: Give great customer service.

"Our commitment is 100 percent to customer service," John Nordstrom once said in a corporate video for new employees. "We are not committed to financial markets, we are not committed to real estate markets, we are not committed to a certain amount of profit. We are only committed to customer service. If we make a profit, that's great. But customer service is first. If I'm a salesperson on the floor and I know that the people that own this place are committed to customer service, then I am free to find new ways to give great customer service. I know that I won't be criticized for taking care of a customer. I will only be criticized if I don't take care of a customer."

KEYS TO SUCCESS

Nordstrom is faced with an enormous number of challenges in the future, including increased competition from a variety of retail store formats, special catalogs, electronic home shopping, exclusive vendor partnerships, and cultural diversity.

In the 1990s, customers' allegiance to a particular store is strongly influenced by their belief that the price they are paying for an item is fair for the value received. One of the ways Nordstrom (like other major retailers) tries to maintain that price/value relationship (and still make a profit) is through private label merchandise, which is available in virtually every product category.

- Nordstrom has become a discounting leader with its Rack stores, which sell end-of-season clearance merchandise.

- Nordstrom is experimenting with a variety of home-shopping formats, including in-home shopping broadcast channels and computer-based on-line services. Nordstrom believes personalized interactive TV shopping is better suited to its brand of customer service because on-screen personal shoppers can directly assist customers.

- To differentiate itself from the competition, Nordstrom is developing exclusive marketing alliances and relationships with a wide assortment of vendors.

- Nordstrom will continue to aggressively expand its retail stores.

- Keeping current good workers with the company is just as important as attracting new ones.

- Greater ethnic diversity of customers, salespeople and suppliers has been a corporate goal since 1987. Today, nearly 30 percent of employees (including 19 percent of management) are people of color.

- Nordstrom has made itself more accessible to disabled customers by developing an employee sensitivity-training program and improving access in the stores. Fashion models with disabilities are featured in catalogs and ads.

- At its best, Nordstrom never forgets that it doesn't have all the answers. They know that the customer has all the information that they need, and that salespeople are the most valuable people in the company.

- Nordstrom's supreme advantage over its competition is that it has been—and will continue to be—controlled and operated by the Nordstrom family. Family control brings an institutional memory, a consistent message and stability for long-range planning.

- The underlying Nordstrom culture and philosophy is not difficult to pass on to the next generation because it's simple: Give great customer service.